The Faery Faith

Serena M. Roney-Dougal

Green Magic

This edition is published by
Green Magic
BCM Inspire
London WC1N 3XX

Typeset by Academic + Technical, Bristol
Printed and bound by Antony Rowe Ltd.

Cover design by Chris Render

Technical assistance
R. Gotto and Richard Fraser

Cover photograph by Gillian Booth © 2002

ISBN 0 9536 6317 5

GREEN MAGIC

DEDICATION

This book is dedicated to all those who love
and care for this beautiful planet, Earth

CONTENTS

COPYRIGHT ACKNOWLEDGEMENTS

I am most grateful to the following for permission to use their illustrations:

Paul Devereux
Mary Evans Picture Library
D. Ford
Brian Froud
Claire Gammon
Leon Gold
Clive Hicks

Esther James
Alan Lee
Kevin Redpath
Willow Roe
Monica Sjöö
Jill Smith

I have made a huge effort to contact people for permission to use their photographs or illustrations. There are some people whom I have failed to find. I do apologise for this and am very happy to pay any dues that may be owed.

ACKNOWLEDGEMENTS

To Tessa Strickland of Gill and Macmillan for initially asking me to write this book – without her impetus it is unlikely it would ever have happened! To Nicholas Mann for inviting me to his book launch where I was introduced to the publishers (thank you Jenny Ashworth who made the introduction!). To Chris and Peter, the publishers, who were happy for me to write it without any deadline pressure whatsoever, and with maximum freedom to do what I want. To Ora, Willow, and all the others who kept encouraging me through the many years confident that it would finally come into being. And to Ora for helping me find some of the illustrations. To Tara Roney-Dougal for helping me find more of the illustrations. To the Bihar Yoga Bharati for inviting me to work at the ashram, where I found the most conducive space for writing. To all at the Society for Psychical Research for helping with the hunt for illustrations, permissions and addresses. To William Bloom, Geoffrey Ashe and Caitlin Matthews for so kindly reading the manuscript, and so generously giving their words, advice and comments. To all my friends and family for their wonderful loving kindness that sustains me so well.

FOREWORD

If you have ever sat in a beautiful spot in the countryside and felt within you a deep tug of something that was not quite memory, not quite recognition, but nevertheless was profoundly moving; if you have ever wondered what process was going on inside of you, then you will enjoy this book. The Faery Faith will lead you into that place between the worlds of here and there where you will begin to comprehend and truly recognize your experience.

Every human being has a wonderful set of senses which give us information: the faculties of sight, hearing, smell, taste and touch are the doors of perception through which we receive vital messages that keep us safe and help us steer through our lives. Equally important are their correlative inner senses – those that most people know as 'the sixth sense:' inner vision, resonance, instinct, discrimination and empathy which provide more subtle knowledge.

Our ancestors knew and used both related sets of senses all the time. They understood that the world is governed by a single reality which has two sides to it and they honoured those who could skilfully perceive and perform spiritual transactions between the two appearances of reality. They acknowledged that the spiritual realm and the physical realm each had its own nature, inhabitants and customs.

Recently we have begun to live in only one side of reality – the side that we call 'the real world' – never realising that we are making ourselves prisoners of an ever shrinking and fearful place that craves the assurance of pre-shrunk knowledge and scientifically verifiable answers. Instead of trusting the wisdom that is inside us and which has been available to the ordinary sensory array of human beings for thousands of years, we are beginning to ignore the information of our senses. The consequence is that we live much less fully and with a significant loss of control and safety, though our logical minds congratulate us on the fact that, having ignored the ancestral mumbo-jumbo of other realms, we are living in better control!

As a shamanic practitioner who is observant of both sides of reality, and understands the consequences of ignoring them, I see very many people in my practice who are like shipwrecked survivors, adrift in a trackless ocean without any compass. In every case, the co-ordinates of their safe homecoming can be found by simple means. It requires that a journey into the timeless present of the otherworld be taken, there to discover that person's daimons or helping spirits who will help reorient, heal or bring wisdom. These spirits are literally co-walkers, those who walk beside us on their side of reality; they take many forms, including those of gods, fairies, animals and ancestors. When such reconnections are made, the injured or straying soul can find its way homeward, and the person in question can begin to live with better respect for the spirits that accompany them.

Serena Roney-Dougal's research into the field of parapsychology has led her to a profound respect for the magical reality that surrounds us all. Her rigorous scientific training sits alongside a great love for the ancient traditions that are the Faery Faith. Such an inclusive welcome to both scientific and magical wisdom is hard to find in today's very polarised society, where to believe in one is often to decry the other. May her book lead you to both question and trust the experiences that you have, and may the wisdom of the Faery Faith conduct you peacefully to the heart of truth!

Caitlín Matthews
29th July 2002
Oxford

INTRODUCTION

It is twelve years since I wrote my first book, *Where Science and Magic Meet*. I think that I am essentially a one-book person, so those of you who have read that tome will recognise in this book certain themes and ideas, and even bits of writing, which are the same. This is because a lot of what I wrote then is still valid, and because some of it is pertinent to the theme of this book. Some people who read that book told me that it was the best cure for insomnia that they had encountered. Essentially I had just written my PhD thesis, and that book came out of it and was written in the same academic style. It is now a decade later and during that time I have been out and about teaching classes and workshops, giving talks and lectures, and generally learning how to communicate in a language which everyone can understand. So this book is my non-academic book, which takes one of themes from *Where Science and Magic Meet* and tells people what I am thinking now. But this is not *Where Science and Magic Meet revised*. It is a new book.

It is a book about fairies. More particularly this is a book about the worldview of people who experience faery reality. It is a book about a philosophy that I think underlies the world's religions from animism and shamanism to the present day pagan revival. When I started studying parapsychology, working with people who were being psychic in the laboratory, I felt that what we were doing was exploring the foundations of religion. Originally religion came out of people's actual experience of the sacred. And psychic phenomena are part of that sacred reality. I felt that in learning what parapsychology has discovered I was learning the fundamentals of a universal spirituality. This is what I call the faery faith.

I don't particularly care for living solely according to belief. I like knowledge and love wisdom, so what I am trying to do here is give you the results of 100 years of scientific research which validates the oldest mystical philosophy of humans. What I love about the scientific method is that it is so careful. The results of just one experiment are not good enough. Something has to be tested over and over again in many different variant ways before one can say with any sense of certainty that this is so, that this we can trust, this is how it is. So science, which literally means knowledge, is something we can rely on to tell us that, from one perspective, this is how the universe is.

When we deal with faery, we are dealing with the world of psyche, with the world of glamour and illusion. I often feel that in the world of the psychic it is a bit like being on a moor just after sunset, in the gloaming, with a mist coming down and you see the faery lights, the fée follets, and they entice you to follow them and in doing so you get lost on the moor and it gets very boggy, and there is every chance you will sink into the bog, and just then you come across a little twisty faery hawthorn tree and you can hold on to it, and where its roots go into the bog the ground is a bit more solid, more stable, it will take your weight. For me parapsychology is that thorn tree. The results of the years of careful research give me a thrill, for I feel it is telling us something very precious, something we need to know in our oh so materialistic society and era, something about magic, about spirit, about our souls. It is food for my soul, just as much as going out into the wild, and being with the moon and the wind and the earth and the sun and the sea, and that spirit of faery feeds me.

So this is my personal philosophy for the 21st century, Western person who is seeking to reconnect with the deeper mystical aspect of their being. I don't want to label this spirituality. It is not witchcraft as most people think of that path – it most certainly is not wicca though many wiccans will finding here knowledge that they will love and consider to be a part of wicca. I like to call it the craft of the wise, because I love wisdom, Sophia, and all that pertains to her, and my present aim is to become a wise woman. A craft is something that takes decades to become adept in – some say it takes 20 years to become a master craftsman, or a mistress of the arts. I'm not talking about a quick fix spirituality, I'm talking about something you grow into with a lifelong dedication and discipline. Many people will find that this philosophy links with some aspects of the neo-pagan revival and that is the closest to a recognised spiritual path that I come. This is why I call it the faery faith, for people have experienced that reality throughout human history and it is to be found as an adjunct to religion everywhere, without actually being a part of any religion.

You will find in this book that science is mixed with faery tales, mixed with personal experiences in my own personal cauldron. I sincerely hope you enjoy reading it as much as I have done living it.

Serena Roney-Dougal

1

Magical Reality and Sacred Sites: The Home of Faery

Faerie or feerie derived from Latin fatare, past participle fae, meaning to enchant (Oxford Dictionary, 1964).[1]

My knowledge of the faery faith stems from my research, as a para-psychologist, into our ability to be aware psychically. This psychic, or psi, awareness is today considered in terms of telepathy, clairvoyance, remote viewing and precognition. In our folklore, the ability to be psychic has been linked with magic, witchcraft and with faeries – the wicked stepmother and the faery godmother being the versions we first hear about through faery stories, when we are very young. They are the chief exponents of magic and the psychic arts. As a child growing up in Scotland, I used to hear of families who had the second sight. Prophecy – the foretelling of events and the future of children, as well as their endowment with certain gifts or qualities – is a typical faery quality. In Scotland, what was known as the second sight was originally regarded as a means of beholding the faeries and only later did the term come to have the meaning of precognition. Robert Kirk, in *The Secret Commonwealth of Elves, Fauns and Faeries* written in 1691,[2] describes how the second sight could be acquired for seeing the faeries, the fair folk, who are magic in their very nature.

The myths and legends of the fair folk are the oldest in Britain and need to be revived. Our culture is like a tree, and as the branches grow higher, so the roots must grow deeper, else we are not properly earthed and all our visions and ideals are just head in the clouds. I think that the British faery tales contain both the patriarchal Celtic mythology, with their warrior heroes, and another older mythology. This mythology I think is pre-Celtic, pre-patriarchal, from the goddess worshipping, Neolithic, shamanic people, of which the witchcraft of Britain was a remnant.

Throughout all times, all people and all cultures there have been those who have believed in and experienced the spirits of the land in

1

Gwynn and the Wild Hunt (Illustration courtesy of Willow Roe.)

which they lived. Some have seen these beings as gods and goddesses, such as Gwynn Ap Nudd (pronounced Neith) whose palace is the entrance to the Welsh underworld, called Annwn, beneath Glastonbury Tor in Avalon. Like Herne the Hunter, he is the leader of the wild hunt, whose white dogs with pink ears and red eyes hunt the souls of the dead. (The word Gwynn is Welsh Brythonic for white, as in Gwynn-ivere, Arthur's wife.) For the underworld of the deities is also the place to which we go when we die, and so is a place of awe, of fear.

Some see these beings as little folk, who can be mischievous, who can help or harm us, who are part of the spirit of the old oak tree, of the apple orchard, like the birds and the flowers, part of the beauty and the wild. Some fear these beings for they can enchant us, cast a glamour over us so that we lose touch with this realm and folks say we are 'gone with the faeries', or 'we've lost it'. Illusion, glamourie is the supreme faery art; transforming one thing into another – a rock into a magnificent castle, leaves into gold, as exemplified so richly in the Cinderella tale.

This aspect of the earth is part of its spirit, part of our spirit, and as our culture gets progressively more and more material, as we become more and more divorced from nature, as the wild places disappear and our lives are lit by bright lights and there is no darkness, no bog, no wild wood, no moorland, so this aspect of our being fades away and is just a tale for children's bedtime.

This belief in faeries, whatever form it takes, is a belief, a world view, a way of living in the world, a philosophy. It is this philosophy that I wish to elucidate in this book. In order to do so, I first have to look at the world view that underpins psychic ability, especially the belief in psychic phenomena and the extent of this realm.

The essence of faery is magic, so let us look a little closer at what this word magic means today. For children, magic is very real. Many children have an invisible companion. Many children see faeries at the bottom of the garden. Faery tales are the language of childhood. It is the language of dreams. As adults we know this reality mainly in our dreams. It is not the reality of our waking world (known to psychologists as secondary process thought), but we can slip in to it lying in the grass on a summer's day, floating in the water at the seaside, going to a good film.

Throughout time many people of many different cultures have consciously entered at will this reality, this mode of thought, for spiritual purposes. These people are called shamanic and they use many different techniques to enter the Otherworld: psychotropic plants, drumming, dancing, chanting, fasting, lack of sleep. Young people in their teens and early twenties seem to have a huge inbuilt urge to go into this consciousness, and so take psychotropic plants, or psychedelic drugs, in order to experience the magic of this reality, of dreamtime, whilst awake.

Parapsychology – the Science of Magic

There has been research over the past 100 years into trance consciousness, into the experience of being psychic. The second sight, the ability to see the future, divination, the ancient magic arts today go by terms such as parapsychology, clairvoyance, telepathy, remote viewing, precognition, psychic healing. They are studied in laboratories and at universities by professors and scientists. They are found to have a certain measure of validity and can be used at will with a certain degree of accuracy. The magic of faery is becoming scientific, coming out of the wild woods, out of the child's tale, and is being measured with statistics. In doing so we are beginning to get a new understanding of ourselves, of our psyches, of our link with spirit and so can bring this world view into our material scientific culture of the 21st century.

The past 100 years of psychical research suggests that we are all psychic all the time; it's not normally conscious, of course, which is why so many people go through life without any awareness of what's going to happen tomorrow. But a lot of people do have dreams which then happen. A lot of people get a feeling that there's something dreadfully wrong only to find that a loved one is badly hurt in an accident; a lot of people get a hunch that if they turn right now they will find a parking place; a lot of people say: 'speak of the devil', as the old friend not seen or heard of for years walks down the street just as they are talking about them. Or you think 'I must phone John' and at that moment the phone rings and John has called you – a good way to keep the phone bill down!

In parapsychology we have found that this subliminal, intuitive, dream mind is the type of consciousness through which we most easily become aware of psychic experiences, through which our psychic awareness most easily influences our actions, our moods, and our thoughts. Research in psychology has found that subliminal perception is in fact occurring 24 hours a day every day of our lives and rules what we think, what we say, what we feel, what we do, and this subliminal perception mode of consciousness has many characteristics which are identical with psychic awareness.

One of the findings of parapsychology is that most psi seems to work through the subliminal mind. We have several layers of mind – the conscious thinking, acting mind is essentially the two cerebral hemispheres, right brain and left brain; the midbrain, thalamus, is the emotional, primary process, instinctive, animal level of mind; the old brain is the on-off switch for body functions, heartbeat, etc.

The subliminal mind as the midbrain mind seems to emerge into consciousness most easily through right hemisphere dream type thought but can emerge directly as a feeling, an emotion, a mood, an intuition, a hunch, a wordless knowing, or a body sensation. Most subliminal perceptions and psychic knowing seem to come through this part of our mind. Its language is symbolic, archetypal as in dreams, collective unconscious, poetry, myths, legends; throughout the world these are the same. When thinking at this level we are linking with the world mind, the mind of the planet.

The unconscious is thought to retain every experience in its entirety. There are literally billions of nerve connections so that physically we can process billions of bits of information all the time: blood flow, heartbeat, glandular secretion, senses. We have filters which protect us from all this, else we would go mad. These are called our defence mechanisms and they protect us from unwanted information so we see and hear what is necessary for our survival, like the big red bus coming down the road at us. Research into subliminal perception has shown that it is the subliminal mind that ultimately governs what we are conscious of. It decides what to let through into consciousness. Our behaviour, our moods, our thoughts, our actions are all governed by the subliminal mind. The filters, the defence mechanisms, are essential but they have tended to become warped in our society so that they now tend to blinker us rather than merely protect us. These filters are originally laid down by the norms of our society and environment. We see only that which we can conceive of. Incredibly basic stuff is controlled by our belief systems and norms of our society.

The subliminal mind is the level at which we can heal or harm others and ourselves as is shown by the placebo effect, psychosomatic illness, or the more dramatic instances of people who create the stigmata on their bodies. It has even been shown through a psychological test called the Defence Mechanism Test that accident proneness is caused by these defences. At a higher level our belief systems, such as whether or not we believe in the psychic, determine whether or not we live with the psychic as part and parcel of our information system on which we base our daily decisions, actions, and moods. Thus people make themselves either lucky or unlucky by unconsciously psychically tuning relevant information in – or out.

Through studying the psychic it has been found that the following psychological aspects are psi-conducive, i.e. are connected with the state most people are in when psi events happen to them:

1. An attitude is the most important action you can take – if you believe in something then it can happen in your life. If you disbelieve in it then even if it does happen you will tend to deny it, this denial occurring a short while after the event happened. Linked with attitude is

expectation – if you expect something to happen it will; create the right atmosphere and the impossible becomes perfectly possible – the trickster, the conjuror is using age-old techniques; the psychic surgeons and shamans create heightened expectation and a charged atmosphere with their rituals and tricks. This allows psi to work better.

2. Relaxation – letting go at every level of your being, both physical and mental relaxation.

3. Concentration – the sort that is best exemplified by a child playing, in which the whole of your being is living the task in which you are engaged, a holistic concentration, totally engrossed in, encompassed by, what you are doing.

4. Visualisation or imagination – essential requirement in all magical traditions and now emerging in science through research into bio-feedback, healing and parapsychology.

5. Emotion – our emotional energy is possibly the strongest energy of our being.

6. Experimenter Effect: whatever we look at we affect; in science the experimenter is the leader in a complex ritual; a social process deeply embedded within a set of symbols and beliefs shared by the actors in the procedure. Many ingredients are attributed to the successful outcome including the dynamics of the group and the physical setting in which the ritual takes place. Thus the person's attitude, personality etc. are vital to the outcome.

7. Working in groups serves to reduce the amount of personal psi responsibility any one person has to take; it shifts the burden of psi onto the group or outside forces. There is a strange reluctance to possess psi abilities oneself and disturbance felt when witnessing them. Both of these anxieties are reduced in group work.

There are many techniques for opening up to the subliminal mind, bringing one's conscious mind into closer contact with the subliminal and its vast store of information, thus helping us grow in knowledge of ourselves, and even potentially contacting our inner wisdom. These techniques are all based around the use of creative imagination together with taking the body/mind into an altered state of consciousness. The dream state is the one most used in both ancient and modern times. Dream induction for psychic and therapeutic purposes is both the most accessible and the most easily realisable of all the techniques. Other traditional shamanic and magical techniques are hypnosis, including self-hypnosis, meditation, and trance. Parapsychology has found that altered states such as hypnosis, meditation and dreaming not only link our conscious minds with our subconscious but also increase psi ability. All the lores of psi are psychological lores.

An everyday example of what is called preconscious awareness is 'the cocktail party' phenomenon in which, across a crowded room of people talking, you hear your name being spoken. Actually you have heard every conversation in that room, but you have screened it out in order to concentrate on the person you are talking with. Your name breaks through into consciousness, whereas all the other conversations are recorded at the subliminal level only. Then there is the subconscious, which where information is recorded by the brain, but you are not even aware that there is anything there. Dixon[3] did a classic experiment in which a person was asked to look at a spot of light on a white screen and, using a knob, to keep this light so it blended in with the screen. The person found that at times the spot became too light and had to be turned down, and at other times became too dark and had to be turned up. What they did not know was that the spot of light was being presented only to one eye. The other eye was being presented with words so fast that the person was completely unaware they were there. But these words affected their ability to see the spot of light. In defensive people, when an emotional word such as penis, whore or cancer was presented, they raised their physiological threshold to the spot of light so that they had to turn the brightness up. With perceptually vigilant people, they lowered their threshold to emotional words, so that the light became too bright and had to be turned down. This is all the subliminal level of mind – occurring without our consciousness awareness at all.

Another example of defensiveness and vigilance occurs using the Poetzl effect.[4] If you see a picture fleetingly, so fast that you do not consciously take it in, you will react in one of two ways to this picture. Imagine it's a nasty picture of a big man about to axe a little boy. One way of reacting is to 'not see' the picture, and if you are shown it for progressively longer times this 'not seeing' means that you have to be shown it for much longer, before you finally consciously see it, than if the picture had been a nice one of a big man giving a little boy a birthday cake. This is called perceptual defensiveness.

The other reaction to a nasty picture is to see it consciously more quickly than one would consciously see the nice picture. This is called perceptual vigilance. This experiment shows us that, at the subliminal level, even when we can't consciously see something, our subliminal mind has seen it, has seen that it is nasty or nice, and has regulated our conscious perception to become aware of the picture or not – to meta-phorically close or open our eyes. This happens all the time. In Sweden they have found that this perceptual defensiveness affects our behaviour, and that people who 'don't see' the nasty picture, have more accidents, are more unlucky. Therefore, all people applying to become pilots in the air

7

force are tested for perceptual defensiveness, because defensive people are more likely to crash their planes – or cars as the case may be.

The same thing occurs in psychic awareness: it is called psi-hitting or luck, if you are vigilant and react to the psychic not-yet-conscious information, such as turning left down the street and finding the parking place; or psi-missing if you always are in the wrong place at the wrong time, and miss the vital appointment because you spent hours looking for the parking place. Douglas Dean[5] wrote a book called *Executive ESP* in which he details famous business men, such as Hilton, who used their sense of 'hunch', or intuition, to run their business and make their millions.

The psi-hitter is the type of person who 'sees' the spirit in the old oak tree under the full moonlight. Psi-miss and you don't even see the tree at all and walk straight into it! Psi-missing is a fascinating process because it means you are psychic, but for various reasons you are defensive about it, and deny the knowledge to the extent that you do the opposite to what your psi information is telling you. Let me try to make this point clearer. Imagine that I flip a coin 100 times and you call heads or tails. By chance you will get it right 50 times because you have a 50/50 chance of being right. But say you get it right 75 times. Now either you are very psychic 'Wow, that's magic', or the coin is fixed! By the same token if you get it right 25 times you are being very psychic but for some reason you are saying the opposite thing every time; you are missing it 75 times.

This defensiveness, this psi-missing, can be caused because you don't believe in the psychic, or you don't believe you are psychic and so you make damn sure that you won't get it right. Or it could be that you are very nervous because there is a sceptic like James Randi breathing down your neck, or you are on television showing how psychic you are, and in such a situation you just can never get it right. Or it could be that you are in a place that is very noisy like Oxford Street, which is totally unconducive to being psychic. So being consciously psychic depends on your beliefs, your environment, your personality, your mood and your state of consciousness. Both subliminal percepts and psi information can be brought into conscious awareness using the same techniques such a meditation, hypnosis and creative visualisation.

An attitude is the most important action you take at the mental level. If you believe something is possible, then it can happen. If you believe in faeries then you have a good chance of experiencing that reality. If you believe something is impossible then it is very unlikely to happen. Very few people who do not believe in faeries ever get to experience that dimension of experience. You may see one, but you are less likely to. So Western people conquering Africa in the 1800s were considered to be incredibly powerful by the witch doctors because they could not easily be hexed. The only reason they could not be hexed was that they did not believe in hexing. The power of their belief protected them. Someone who doesn't believe in psychic ability does not experience it. Some of our attitudes are very deeply seated and colour our whole personality and our lives. Most of our attitudes are formed in childhood, primarily from our families, then from our social milieu, e.g. working class, landed gentry; then from our cultural background, e.g. Scottish, southern; then from our nationality – the Italians are very different from Scandinavians in their national temperament, outlook and attitudes. This is the power of our imagination and belief systems, and is the foundation of the faery faith: belief in psychic reality, that the mental world is as real as that of the physical.

Linked to this is an effect known as the experimenter effect. Just as some people have psychic effects happening in their lives, some experimenters have psychic effects in their laboratory studies most of the time and some never have it happen. This seems to be a mixture of attitude and personality.

Obviously if you go into a laboratory to do experiments on your psychic ability, then a warm, friendly, psi-conducive atmosphere will help, whereas a cold, clinical attitude will hinder. This effect can happen at a distance (i.e., psychically) as well. An experiment in the 1950s was done in which two people (Fisk & West[6]) each shuffled a deck of cards. About twenty people were sent two sheets of paper on which they were asked to guess the order of the cards which had been shuffled, not knowing that two different people had shuffled a pack each. The participants, in their own time, guessed the order of the cards for each of the two sheets and sent them back. When the results were analysed it was found that the participants successfully guessed the order of the cards for one of the experimenters (Fisk) but not for the other (West). One was a psi-conducive experimenter and one was not – and this effect manifested psychically. Recently Schlitz,[7] a psi-conducive experimenter, teamed up with Wiseman, a psi-negative experimenter, doing remote staring experiments and found exactly the same thing.

It takes a little time to realise the implication of this study. It means that if we do not let psi happen around us, even at a distance with people who do not know we are involved, this psi-negative effect can still happen. So in our western culture with all the city people, the scientific and establishment people saying there is no such thing as the psychic, it's a wonder that anyone has psychic experiences in their lives, or in experiments, at all. I think that this effect is occurring globally. When anthropologists first started interviewing shamans back in the 1800s they were shown fantastic phenomena, but all the shamans said that what they could do was nothing compared with what their ancestors had done. By the 1800s the rational West had already decided that there was no such thing as psychic phenomena, that it was just superstitious nonsense. I think that this attitude of the Western culture had psychically influenced people who had never had any physical connection with the West, that the global ability to experience psi was diluted and diminished by Western scepticism. Our culture has literally frightened away the faeries!!

Personality has to be taken into account when understanding why some people have the second sight and experience of faery and some do not. This is something that has been noticed again and again in parapsychology. Some people are successful experimenters, some people are star subjects, some people can never find any sign of psychic experience in their research, some people show not a hint of psychic ability.

People have looked at factors such as extroversion and introversion, at how neurotic people are, anxiety levels, and so far the best that has been suggested is that psychics who do well in experiments tend to be musical, artistic, 'sensitive' people; the sort who are not very at home in the world of commerce, accounts, tax, government and the military. Now this is about as vague as one can get, and it's that sort of personality. People who are susceptible to being hypnotised are those who tend to have psychic experiences, and the more susceptible one is the more one is likely to report having had psychic experiences. So if you are a dreamer, an artist, a musician, if you have had peak experiences, mystical experiences, flying or lucid dreams, then you are more likely to have psychic experiences.

There are certain states of consciousness that are conducive to magic. And there are certain times and places that are conducive to being psychic. Night time is the traditional time for magic. The Victorians found that the dark is most conducive to mediums manifesting ectoplasm and other spirit pranks, although some mediums, like D.D. Home, always worked in light. There has been very little research into this, but one study done in India suggests that 3 a.m. is more conducive to psi awareness than is 9 p.m. Certainly folklore says that you are more likely to see faeries at night, that witches work their magic at night, that midnight is the witching hour, the time when Cinderella must leave the ball.

The Pineal Gland: Third Eye and Psychic Chakra

My research into the pineal gland, reputed by Descartes to be the seat of the soul, considered by yogis to be the physical location of ajna chakra

The Shamanic - Pineal Link

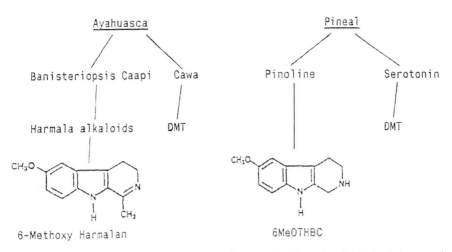

The chemical diagram shows the similarity between the harmala alkaloid of the sacred vine in Ayahuasca and pinoline made by the pineal gland.

(the psychic centre), by Theosophists to be the third eye, suggests that night-time really is the psychic time *par excellence*. If you want to discover the full story it is presented in detail in my book *Where Science and Magic Meet*.[8] For now I shall summarise that information, because it is central to my understanding of the faery faith and its recent resurgence in modern paganism.

The pineal gland only produces its chemicals when it is dark. It starts up at sunset and stops at dawn; it is a creature of the night! It reaches peak production six hours after dusk, being a bit of a slow starter, like me in the morning. Which means it reaches peak production after midnight – the magic or witching hour. And by 3–4 a.m. it is going full speed ahead. This is the time when Buddhists meditate, when yogis rise to start their practices, when monks get up to chant the Matins, the time when the veils are thin, when this world and that of spirit are very close, when most people die, if they are allowed to die naturally, and when most babies are born.

One of the chemicals made by the pineal gland is called melatonin – it's a neurohormone and the neuro bit works on the brain to send us to sleep, so that a few hours after sunset we are sleepy and ready for bed. This is part of our biological clock that runs on the circadian (sun) rhythm. The other chemical made by the pineal is called pinoline, and it is thought to act on a major neurochemical in the brain, serotonin; the end result being to create a hallucinogen called DMT.

DMT is a very powerful psychedelic, which is very fast acting and short lived. One suggestion that has been made is that this is the neuro-chemical trigger for dreaming. Dreaming is a hallucinogenic state of consciousness and is one of the states that has been found in parapsychology to be very psi-conducive. The majority of reports of spontaneous psychic experiences describe these experiences as happening at night, whilst asleep or dreaming. I am very interested in the link between psychic phenomena and our physical state. The mind and body are inextricably linked whilst we are alive and living on this earth. Everything we do to the body affects the mind, as anyone who needs a cup of coffee in the morning knows. And everything that goes on in the mind affects the body. In para-psychology, we are slowly but surely becoming increasingly clear that an altered state of consciousness helps one to become consciously aware of psychic experiences. To me, this earthing of spiritual knowledge actually helps me to understand it better.

The dream state of consciousness is the state that very young children are in: the primary process state as it is called by psychology, the world of faerytale, of seeing wolves under the bed, faeries at the bottom of the garden, when 'teddy' talks to you and you to him. The dream state is now thought to be the state we slip into whenever we shut down the senses. Close your eyes and relax. If you are not tense, are not anxious, if your 'monkey mind' can slow down and your thoughts stop spinning, you enter the dream world. This is the basic training for psychics – to connect with our normally subconscious mind, that subliminal mind which is the first to be aware of information and which ultimately controls who we are. This is the state of conscious-ness that magicians work with. This is the state in which we connect with faery.

It is the state of consciousness that shamans use. In classic shamanism, when the shamans are working to heal someone, they enter an altered state of consciousness. They also do this to divine the future, or to travel in their spirit body (out-of-body as we call it, or astral travelling), in order to see things or effect things at a distance. To do this many use psychotropic plants. In the Amazon region all the tribes use ayahuasca, known also as yagé or caapi.

The chemicals in ayahuasca are very similar to pinoline, the chemical made by the pineal gland, which suggests that pinoline and its interaction with serotonin, not only takes us into the dream type state of conscious-ness, but is actually specifically psi conducive. It also suggests that use of ayahuasca in some way mimics what occurs naturally for us every night. I think that every night, every person experiences a shamanic state of consciousness in which they can leave their body and travel in the spirit world.

1. The conventional witch
   a. Fourteenth century, from Lyon Cathedral
   b. Seventeenth century: Jennet Dibb and her cat
   c. Nineteenth century: the crone on a broomstick
   d. Twentieth century: the Walt Disney version

It is interesting to see how the images of witches over the last 700 years retain some aspects whilst others change. (Illustration reproduced from Witchcraft *by Pennethorne Hughes, Penguin, 1932/1970.)*

The shamans of Britain were called wise women, or witches, and cunning men or magicians. They were the healers, the astrologers; people said that they could fly. They knew about herbs and plants, and the witch's ointment, called the flying ointment, is a psychoactive ointment consisting of belladonna, henbane, mandrake and datura (thorn apple). This mixture is known to facilitate a mental state suitable for out-of-body experiences. This ritual is preserved in the children's nursery rhyme:

> Ride a cock horse to Banbury Cross,
> To see a fine lady upon a white horse,
> With rings on her fingers and bells on her toes,
> She shall have music wherever she goes.

Belladonna in combination with aconite is also known to produce falling dreams in sleeping people, so the belief that the witches actually physically flew is a folk memory of the out-of-body art of shamanic people. It has been suggested that they only resorted to these drugs during the centuries of persecution when they could not meet together for fear of indictment, but the fact that the use of psychoactive plants is the norm amongst shamanic peoples would suggest that the traditional people of Britain knew and used these herbs for psychic and spiritual purposes.

This use of local herbs for their psychoactive properties is a link between witchcraft with the shamanism of other continents, especially the Americas where the shamans use a vast variety of different plants for their healing and psychoactive properties. The out-of-body experience is in fact common to shamanic cultures over most of the Northern Hemisphere, the Lapland and Siberian version being the origin of our Santa Claus myth, a wonderful tale which I shall digress to tell.

The word shaman comes from the Tlingit people of Siberia who herd reindeer. They used fly agaric (*Amanita muscaria*) mushrooms for shamanic purposes, and these also induce an out-of-body experience. A woodcut of these people shows the shaman in the hide teepee lying flat on the ground whilst someone watches over him, with his drum laid on his body to protect him. He was understood to have flown up through the smoke hole at the top of the lodge, and to then return through the smoke hole, just as did the witches through the chimney. These people found that reindeer also eat fly agaric mushrooms and that, if they drank reindeer urine, they would have the psychedelic effects without the awful nausea or dangerous side effects you can get from eating fly agaric mushrooms. So Santa Claus is an ancient mushroom eating shaman, dressed in red and white to symbolise the mushrooms, and he flies with a reindeer because the reindeer are flying

The original Santa Claus flying with Rudolph: a wonderful example of a modern fairy tale with clear roots in animistic shamanism (Illustration courtesy of Claire Gammon.)

on mushroom juice too. He brings back gifts from the elves and the pixies at the north pole, because as the shaman he can travel to the spirit world, the otherworld, the world of the faeries, and bring back gifts of wisdom, knowledge or healing.

Electricity – the Link Between Psyche and Matter

All matter is a complex interweaving of charges and fields; all matter is both electric and magnetic. Electromagnetism seems to be the interface between body and mind, between physical and spiritual. It is not the chi energy of the Chinese, or mana of the Philippine people, or prana, but is related to them. Let us look more closely at the strange properties of electricity and magnetism, since they are linked with many a magical idea for which we have as yet had no down to earth explanation, and my contention is that all magical ideas have very real psychological and physical earth-based reasons.

Electricity is the nerve that energises matter, life and society. It is the physical aspect of the life force. Light from the stars is their life force reaching through the universe. Ball lightning, UFOs, ley lines, dowsing, sacred sites, psychic phenomena can all be linked using our knowledge of electromagnetic energy. This is not to reduce these phenomena to the purely physical, but to be a starting point for a fresh way of looking at them and seeing the common ground between them all. I see the scientific approach as being one facet of the whole, one aspect of our understanding that complements and grounds the mystical, magical and esoteric levels of understanding.

The body is electric[9]. Some people are supersensitive to electricity. Some people disrupt electrical equipment such as blowing light bulbs, and are liable to be struck by lightning. These people are often psychic. Several poltergeist cases have involved electrical craziness. For example, in the 1960s in Rosenheim, Germany, a young girl affected the telephone, the light bulbs, the electricity meter and other electrical equipment in the office where she worked so that eventually she had to leave.

Some consider that the aura is this electric body-field surrounding all living matter. Harold Saxton Burr[10] called it the Life or L-field. Others call it the etheric body, or the energy body, or the pranic body. This electric field regulates the growth and pattern, and maintains the structure, of the being during its life. It is the mechanism by which the wholeness, organisation and continuity of life are maintained. Burr monitored trees over a 30 year period and found that trees display a daily L-field rhythm, peaking at midday with a minimum at night. Tree growth follows this pattern. Changes in electric field were found to be due to fluctuations in the local environment and followed a lunar and a seasonal pattern. The 11-year sunspot cycle is also evident. Thus, the electric field of all living things is affected by the environment. Electrically all things are interrelated: the stars, the sun, the moon, the planets, the earth and all its inhabitants. We are electric creatures living in an electric world.

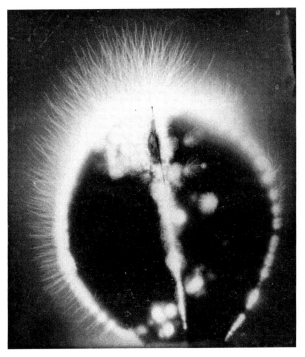

Kirlian photograph showing the electrical corona discharge around a leaf. (Illustration courtesy of Leon Gold.)

Some people consider that our electric body alters when we get ill, and that Kirlian photography records this. It is well known from psycho-somatic medicine that mental stress results in physical disorder. Emotional states can be equated with energy. The electrical skin response (known as the EDA), used in parapsychological and in subliminal perception research, shows that electrical changes occur in the skin correlating with emotions, thoughts and level of stress, of tension and relaxation. This is the direct connection between our psyche and electromagnetism, and highlights our sensitivity to changes in our environment. It is a two-way process, our emotional state affects our body's electric field, and our body electricity affects our emotional and mental state.

Earth Magic: the Pineal and the Earth's Magnetic Field

If something is to have effect on this earth plane then at some point it has to 'shift through' into physical form, and the electromagnetic seems to be the linking energy. One of the intriguing things about my research with

17

the pineal gland is that it can help us to understand why we have psychic, mystical and magical experiences in sacred places. As already mentioned, the pineal gland is switched on by the dark. It is also affected by the earth's magnetic field (geomagnetic field – GMF). Changes in GMF strength affect the production of certain of the chemicals that make melatonin and serotonin, and hence the pinoline which appears to be connected with a psi-conducive state of consciousness.

In parapsychology it has been found that when the GMF is more intense than normal, that this is related to people reporting poltergeist or apparitional type of experiences, and to enhanced success with healing experiments in the laboratory – what I call active psi. There was a long term series of experiments run by William Braud and Marilyn Schlitz[11] in which they investigated the effects of distant healing (distant mental influence on living systems (DMILS) or bio-PK, as they called it). They measured the person's skin electricity (EDA) and found that it responded to another person watching or thinking about them. This healing effect was stronger when the GMF was more intense than normal.

When the GMF decreases in intensity this is related to more people reporting telepathic and clairvoyant type of experiences (what I call receptive psi), and to these sorts of experiments having greater success in the laboratory. For example, remote viewing,[12] which has recently become much talked about because of the United States military programme investigating the possibility that people could 'spy' psychically, seems to be more successful when the GMF is quieter than normal. Remote viewing is a mixture of clairvoyance, telepathy and precognition, very like the shamanic travelling without the experience of leaving one's body. So our psychic experiences appear to be related in some way to changes in the GMF.

We are very sensitive to the GMF in many other ways. For instance it seems that we have a magnetic sense of direction. Robin Baker[13] at Manchester University blindfolded a coach load of students, the windows of the coach also being blacked out. The coach was then driven for twenty minutes in a twisting turning route and at the end the students were taken out, spun around and asked to point to where they had come from. In general, more or less, the students were able to do so, but if magnets were placed within the blindfold, by their temples, they completely lost their sense of direction and pointed at random. This was followed up by a student of Baker's (Gail Murphy) who took young children, sat them in a chair that could spin, in a darkened room and asked them to point north. Only after puberty and amongst girls who were willing to give up and guess were the children able to do this. This aspect of only getting it correct by not using the logical, analytical, conscious mind is a typical trait of subliminal information. And the GMF is certainly subliminal!! Exactly what in our bodies or brains allows us to have this subliminal magnetic sense of direction is still open to question. A fact that I find intriguing, is that at puberty the bridge of our nose grows (calcifies), and at the same time the pineal gland calcifies. Perhaps, with its extreme sensitivity to changes in the GMF, the calcified pineal is also implicated in our sense of direction.

Changes in the GMF are linked with many variables, the strongest of which is the sunspot cycle. When there are strong solar flares, these create magnetic storms on earth known as the Northern Lights. However, the magnetic field changes in less obvious ways all the time, one regular cause of variation being the moon, and recent research by Dean Radin[14] suggests that the full moon enhances telepathy, and whatever psi ability we use when gambling. A four year study of a casino in Las Vegas found that all slot machine jackpots occurred at the full moon, and winnings at roulette, blackjack, etc., occurred more frequently on days either side of the full moon. So both the GMF and the moon seem to be linked with our psychic ability.

Research into dowsing suggests that in some circumstances, such as water dowsing or dowsing for minerals, the dowser is being sensitive to slight changes in the GMF, caused by the geological fault line in which the water is flowing, or in which the seam of ore is found. Dowsing seems to be more than just this GMF sensitivity, however. Research by a German water aid group in Sri Lanka,[15] where many wells are being dug, has found that a water dowser (Hans Schröter) could successfully predict the best place in which to dig a well, for the maximum water flow and the depth at which the well should be dug, 94% of the time. Geophysical equipment was accurate only 60% of the time, so the dowser was much more efficient than the equipment. One suggestion is that the dowser uses psychic awareness as well as GMF awareness, both of these being subliminal information to which he has learnt to be sensitive, and has had sufficient experience to translate into the useful skill of well digging.

The Electrical Nature of Stone

The earth is a giant bar magnet. There is an electric current running through the earth's crust which is linked to the GMF. Rocks are formed from the earth's molten magma which cools when it erupts on to the surface, solidifying and its components becoming aligned with the GMF as it is at that time and place, and so forming a record of our planet's magnetic history. Since the GMF is constantly changing, the rocks have an induced magnetism due to the GMF at that time. Rocks with a high proportion of magnetic minerals, primarily those of iron, will have a higher magnetic susceptibility. The GMF is linked with the electrical properties of the solar system.

The important point to remember from this is that some rocks have unusual magnetic strength, others have very little, and they are all oriented in different directions. Thus we live on an electrical and magnetic planet, which permeates the rocks of the crust on which we walk and thereby affects the surrounding atmosphere. There is a suggestion that we are sensitive to these ground changes in orientation of magnetic field as well as to the north–south direction of the GMF. Changes in the orientation of the field affects the pineal gland, as do changes in intensity. We are exquisitely sensitive to this magnetic field of the earth.

We are affected by rocks of different ages if there is a sudden change, say at a geological fault line where two rocks of different ages meet, or where there is what is called a surface intrusion (in which a rock of a different age pushes up through a surrounding rock), because we get anomalous GMFs at these places. Stresses on geological faults create electric and magnetic effects through the piezoelectric effect. Piezoelectricity is the property by which pressure on a crystalline object causes a static electric field – as in electronic lighters. Those of you who have gas cookers and have 'piezoelectric lighters', are using this effect of squeezing a crystal in order to get a spark, and you will notice the crackle at the same time. Very high charges can be built up in quartz crystals which, when discharged, give off a mini version of thunder and lightning.

Hair becomes charged and stands on end if touched by an electrostatic item. As a child did you ever comb your hair by a radio and listen to the static? It also stands on end if you go into a haunted house, suggesting that the place has some unusual electrostatic properties. And the classic time to see a ghost is during a lightning storm! There was a television programme on ghosts in Britain, in which they stated that there are more reported apparitions in Britain and Ireland than in any other countries in the world, about one in ten people seeing a ghost at least once in their life. That's about 6 million people in Britain who have seen a ghost, which is a lot of ghosts wandering around. One thing that stands out in these reports is that the sounds, sights, smells, touch, and temperature changes experienced in haunting, are all similar to those reported in connection with lightning, the aurora borealis, and strong static electricity.

Could the supposed magical properties of quartz, silicon, amber, bone, feather, fingernails, hair and other crystals be related to their electrostatic properties? Is the calcified pineal piezoelectric?

Sacred Stones: Stone Circles and the Earth's Magnetic Field

There are certain places where the world of faery is strongest. These are the wild places, the woods and moorlands, these are the stone circles, the barrows and tumuli, these are the sacred sites. What is it about such places that make them so charged? Hundreds of thousands of people flock to Glastonbury every year because of the atmosphere of the place, which they love and which affects them strongly. Some people refuse to come here because they are too strongly affected so that they find it difficult. Some people who come here to live have to leave because their lives are turned upside down. This place is a myth a moment – layers and layers of mythology overlay the land. So many places in Britain are associated with the fair folk.

The West coast of Britain – Cornwall, Wales, Cumbria and Scotland – are all areas of intense geological faulting and magnetic anomalies. These are the very areas where you get the majority of the ancient sites, ley lines, UFO sightings and people with 'second sight'. There is a strong folklore linking stone circles, other sacred sites and ley lines with psychic

The stones at Avebury are magical, awesome in their size, and create a very special atmosphere. (Illustration courtesy of Esther James.)

21

events, people who live in these areas having 'second-sight', apparitions, haunted houses, faery legends and so on. Psychically they are the most 'charged' area of Britain. From the research done into the enormous number of henges, mounds, and stone complexes that they built, it appears that the stone circles highlight a megalithic science whose essence is the conjoining of nature and psyche. So let me present here for you my latest understanding of what the energies involved in the circles are, and how they link to the psychic realm.

Our sensitivity to geological fault lines seems to be part of what I call megalithic science. 80% of the stone circles in Britain are built within a mile of a geological fault line. Many of the stones in these circles show magnetic anomalies. The Dragon Project[16] in the 1970s measured some of the stone circles in Britain. One of the places with which they worked extensively were the Rollright stones. These have many magnetic stones and also a fascinating folk lore.

This complex comprises a large circle of about seventy stones, called the King's Men, of which it is said that it is impossible to count them. Once a baker went round putting a loaf on each stone so as to count them that way, but he didn't have enough loaves! There is also a group of five large stones, called the Whispering Knights, which once formed a chamber, and there is a large single megalith called the King Stone. The legend says that all these stones were once human beings, as is also said about the Merry Maidens in Cornwall, but in this case they are reputed to have been a king and his army who were marching across the land when they were met by a witch who said to the king:

'Seven long strides shalt thou take.
If Long Compton thou canst see
King of England thou shalt be.'

The king's reply was:

'Stick, stock, stone,
As King of England I shall be known'

But when he had taken the seven strides all he could see was the Arch-druids Barrow, a natural mound which has now been ploughed out, which blocked his view of the village in the valley below. So he and his men were turned into stone by the witch:

'As Long Compton thou canst not see,
King of England thou shalt not be.
Rise up stick, and stand still stone,
For King of England thou shalt be none.
Thou and thy men hoar stones shall be
And myself an eldern tree.'[17]

(b) *Geological faults in Great Britain. Only the major faults are illustrated. (P. McCartney.) If you imagine laying one map over the other, you see how closely the two mirror each other. (Illustrations courtesy of Paul Devereux. Reproduced from Earthlights by Paul Devereux, Turnstone Press, 1982.)*

(a) *Stone circles in Great Britain. Notice the high concentration in the north and west of the country, and their total absence in the south east.*

The faery aspect of this story is connected with the role of the witch since in olden time the witches were people who could converse with the fair folk, who sometimes even married fair folk, and who received their magic abilities from these beings, so in as much as the witch created the circle this is by the art and power of the fair folk from whom she derived her power. This is exemplified by her turning into an elder tree, this tree being one of the sacred trees much respected for its link with faery magic. I have noticed that quite often a witch is referred to when the story could equally refer to one of the fair folk.

The story surrounding the Merry Maidens stone circle in Cornwall is another classic in that it is supposed to be a circle of women who went dancing on a Saturday night and carried on after midnight, at which time a faery musician appeared and the music was such that they just couldn't stop dancing and carried on until cockcrow, when the faery disappeared and they were turned to stone. Two standing stones nearby are called 'the pipers'.

These are places where the magnetic field is more intense, so we have what I call 'active psi' experiences: we see apparitions, we hear faery music. I suspect that they are good places for healing. I suspect that poltergeist, haunting type experiences happen there. For those who like to practise active magic these are the power spots.

Comprehensive maps in Paul Devereux's book *Earthlights*,[18] which tells of findings from the Dragon Project, show the relationship between stone circles and geological faulting. Of the 286 stone circles in Britain today, 235 of them are found on Pre-Armorican rock outcrops. (Pre-Armorican rocks are those that are more than 250 million years old and cover 36% of the land mass of Britain.) There is less than a one in a million chance that the stone circles were placed on these specific rock outcrops at random. These rocks are extensively faulted causing localised changes in intensity of the GMF. Paul Devereux and the Dragon Project recorded all sorts of phenomena at the Rollright Stones in Oxfordshire using gaussmeters, infrared cameras, ultrasonic detectors, dowsing and Geiger counters, which have shown anomalous magnetic readings near the stones.

In old crystalline granites such as make up many of the stone circles, the stone is formed of a mixture of different types of quartz. Don Robins,[19] from the Dragon Project, suggests that these highly crystalline stones in standing stones and stone circles act as condensers. In a condenser the electric charge gets stored until something specific happens, when the electricity discharges with a cracking spark. The stones seem to be discharged when the dawn light first hits them. Several well-known and respected dowsers have also measured unusual effects which tally with this magnetic and also with radioactive data.

Thus the Neolithic people not only chose very specific places for the stone circles, places of unusual magnetic field strength, but they also chose very specific stones to build the circle with, many of these stones having their own unusual magnetic fields. Both place and stone have properties that enhance active psi effects.

The stone circles have also been found to have other strange physical properties. At Rollright audiosonic equipment measured a high pitched sonic outburst from the stones just at the moment of dawn; and infrared photography showed a burst of infrared from the stones at the same time. This effect has also been noticed by ornithologists recording bats near to ancient sites. So there is some interaction between the stone and the energising effect of light first hitting it – just as in the film '2001: A Space Odyssey'. Radioactive levels have been measured with a Geiger counter and certain areas around sites have yielded above-average counts. It appears that an ionisation effect is being recorded, which tallies with Don Robins' ideas concerning the condenser effect of stone. Paul Devereux discusses this in depth in his book, *Places of Power*.[20]

This research corroborates ideas that the energy, which dowsers are picking up, is linked to geomagnetic energies, that wax and wane according to the cycles of the sun, moon and other planets. In other words, because many of the British stone circles are built on quartz-bearing granite intrusions, and are themselves built out of ancient quartz bearing stone, the whole circle is surrounded by unusual geomagnetic fields, and static electric, sonic and infrared discharges occur when such activity as dawn, or hand pressure, touches the stones. Because we are electromagnetic beings, we obviously interact with the electrical energies of the stones, and touching them causes pressure on them so that an electrical discharge occurs, similar to the piezoelectric effect. This could be the cause of the folk lore of people being violently thrown back from the stones, the stones dancing, and the legends of them walking to the nearby river or sea at certain times of the year or phases of the moon.

It is very possible that the megalithic builders observed the energies of the places over many centuries before they started building the circles and that the shape of the circle and the placing of the stones is determined by the energy of the place as much as by the alignments to sunrise, sunset, moon rise and other astronomical events. Silbury Hill is 130 feet high; there are thousands of barrows and other earthworks and nearly 300 stone circles. Work on these sites covered thousands of years. The Neolithic people were not crude barbarians! What will our civilisation have still remaining in 5000 years' time? Attempted renovation at Avebury showed that, even with modern machines, erecting these huge stones was a mammoth task. The centuries-long construction of the major monuments tells us that the PLACE was the important factor, since at Stonehenge the Bronze Age peoples added to what the Neolithic had started. Bringing in bluestones from Wales – over 200 miles journey – shows that MATERIAL was as important as place. Henges seem to be temples, astronomical observatories and even universities. Scientific and magical functions seem to be inextricably interwoven. And knowing what we do now about the effect of the earth's magnetic field on psychic functioning we realise that these places and the stones were specially chosen for enhancement of magical working.

Barrows – Ancient Energy Accumulators?

Associated with the stone circles are the barrows, the tumuli, the traditional home of the fair folk. The round barrows are traditionally home of the fair folk, such as the Faery Toot near Nempnet Thrubwell in Somerset, which has been ploughed out now, but still has a huge ash tree over the entrance with roots that form a giant hand protecting and guarding the old entrance. A picture of it drawn by a Victorian antiquarian before it was ploughed shows it to have been what is called a stalled cairn, with about 20 chambers. A barrow called Elf Howe in Yorkshire and another at Beedon in Berkshire were also said to be inhabited by faeries.[21] Barrowwall barrow at Carn Gluze near St. Just in Cornwall has a tradition of faeries dancing on it and a friend of mine who spent Hallowe'en there one year (this is the Celtic New Year called Samhain) saw the shadows of them dancing as he played his flute. They even knocked out one of his hurricane lamps, which made him play just that little bit more animatedly!! Nothing like scaring humans to get their attention and get them to play music you can dance wildly to! An old English chap book shows the faeries dancing. On the left of the picture is a faery hill or fort as they are called, which is the shape of a tumulus. This is the classic picture of a faery fort, so take note of its shape because this is important later.

Have you ever spent a night in one of these places? It is so beautiful. Let me tell you of one of my experiences because I just love spending time meditating in barrows, and one summer I was on a holiday travelling around Ireland with my two daughters. We were coming back east and I had been told to visit the cairns at Lough Crew which is in Gaelic called 'The hill of the Cailleach', the cailleach being the hag form of the goddess, the old crone. These chambered cairns are said to be 6500 years old, said to be the oldest megalithic barrows in Europe.

The Fairy Toot at Nempnett Thrubwell (illustration courtesy of D. Ford.)

There are about ten of them on top of the hills and at sunset we climbed up the hill with the key to a cairn that is still intact. We set up our tent on top of the hill amongst all the ruined barrows and went inside the cairn. It is so beautiful, full of carvings on the walls. Because it was Lammas (Lughnasadh, the Celtic festival to mark the end of summer and the beginning of autumn, the beginning of the harvest) we chanted a few songs as the night drew in, and then my oldest daughter started to feel a bit spooked, so I took them into the tent and tried to settle them down as best I could. I then left them to go and meditate in the end chamber of the cairn – the one that my eldest daughter saw as having a zodiac carved in the roof, although it is no zodiac that I have ever seen depicted anywhere else. There I sat with my blanket over my shoulders in the dark of the night. How long I sat I have no idea. I suddenly found myself in a space that I can only describe as the space between the galaxies. It felt like I was in an intergalactic telephone exchange, crazy though that sounds. The utter silence of deep space, the total peace that knows no bounds. And I heard a voice – it told me I had a choice. I could either step through into another dimension – faery-land as I know it – or I could go back. Now sadly for me I was brought up with the Celtic tales rather than the C. S. Lewis' tales of Narnia.[22] In

Faeries dancing by a remarkably UFO-like tumulus, with a fly agaric mushroom, and a green man in the tree — all classic symbology. To me the faeries look ever so like witches with their pointy hats. (Illustration from a 17th century chapbook. Reproduced from Fortean Times, R.J. Rickard and P. Sieveking (eds.), 1989, 53, p.45.)

the Celtic tales a night and a day in faeryland is a year and a day on earth — the Rip Van Winkle effect as I call it. Rip Van Winkle came across some fair folk partying and decided to join them for the weekend. But when he returned to his village after the party was over everyone he knew had died long ago and his children now had grandchildren. 75 years had passed on this earth whilst he had spent a few nights and days with the fair folk. So there was no way I could step through into faeryland, because my children were there in the tent amongst all the barrowights and I couldn't leave them. I had no choice and with a bump I found myself back in my body sitting in the chamber with my blanket round my shoulders. How long I had been out I had no idea. I sat there wondering what to do next, when I noticed the wall at the end of the chamber facing the passageway glowing bright orange and then going dark again, as if illuminated by car headlights. Or so I thought. It happened again, and then again and slowly it dawned on me that I was at the end of a twenty foot passage in a cairn on top of a hill hundreds of feet above the nearest road, that it was late at night and there was no way car headlights could illuminate the end wall of the chamber. And anyway the light was not casting my shadow on the wall. This was a bit too spooky for me. I felt that I was being asked to leave, so, mustering all my dignity, I folded my blanket, picked up my rug and without looking behind me walked slowly to the entrance, locked the gate and looked up into the starry night sky. At that moment the largest shooting star I have ever seen, described an arc in the sky before me and then blew out. Fantastic experience! I do recommend it to you.

Barrows generally have large stones creating the passage and chambers, around which are layers of earth, clay, gravel, and often faced with quartz chips. It is now known that some Bronze Age tumuli are built of clays that are not local, showing that the material used in even these little, exceedingly common structures was of vital importance. These clays, built sandwiched between an inner stone layer and the outer grass covering, act to shield the inside of the chamber from geomagnetic fields. The feeling is identical to that experienced inside a Faraday chamber, which is made from fine copper mesh and screens out electromagnetic radiation.

Thus the composition of barrows is that of layers of organic and inorganic materials, which reduces ambient electromagnetic fields in a similar manner to modern Faraday chambers, or Reichian orgone chambers.[23] This reduction in electromagnetic fields is linked with psychic awareness to create an environment conducive to clairvoyance or telepathy, for receptive psi which seems to be maximised by a reduction in GMF strength. So it really does seem as if there was some sort of neolithic psychic technology. Barrows are found all over the world and they all have the same pattern of construction. Some tumuli have been found with fire pits in the centre but no wood fire. Instead blackened pieces of stones are found.[24] This suggests a sweat lodge where heated stones are placed in the fire pit. As there was no smoke hole this would make complete sense. Recent connection with American Indian spiritual tradition where sweat lodges are commonly used, would suggest that the Neolithic peoples used these tumuli as sweat lodges, which makes me feel that different tumuli and barrows had different functions as meditation chambers, places for all night vigil, for out-of-body inductions, initiation chambers, and so on. In fact many years ago, I remember reading about a barrow that was found with a circle of skeletons inside it, and the thought was that they had been astral travelling and something had happened so that they died and were interred in the barrow.

I think they were places for initiation into the art of travelling from this world to the otherworld in full consciousness. But not for mothers with responsibility to their children – for initiates who were dedicated to spiritual growth and could travel in such a manner, who could disappear in faeryland for whatever time was appropriate. These are all initiation places much as the Tibetan lamas and the yogis would go into a cave for whatever time was deemed necessary for meditation in order to attain enlightenment. This is the relic of our Western tradition that is so very similar in its essentials to the Eastern practices.

Seeing the otherworld is dependent on being able to see with one's mind's eye. I had the experience one night when the moon was full of going to a local sacred grove, and as I stood under the yew tree looking into the clearing I could see the faery queen, and the faeries were having a ball, dancing giddy in circles. And then I looked with my day eyes and saw moonlight on the leaves. I preferred the faery ball and switched back into my other eyes and once again watched them dancing. David Peat[25] has described how the Blackfoot Indians say our ability to perceive the otherworlds requires that our minds be soft, be weak, not critical, not bound by the senses, but sensitive to vision, to dream, to play as children do.

Emotion is vital in a magical or psychic event. Hauntings by specific ghosts tend to be connected with traumatic life events, or a traumatic death, of the particular apparition. This means that there is a lot of emotional energy surrounding the life/death circumstances of the apparition. If a place is charged by unusual geomagnetic fields, and the people living in that intense place react intensely, then it is hypothesised that this emotional energy in some way affects their energy body and that this imprints on to the surrounding earth field of the place, just as radio waves carrying information can be picked up with crystal receivers. Thus you get the same ghostly action occurring repeatedly as a memory replay imprinted onto that particular energy field, which, like a film, can be rerun for those who are sensitive enough to pick up the atmosphere of the place – atmosphere is an interesting word in this context, in so far as it denotes weather condition, air pressure – and emotional states. Our language again and again points out these underlying connections between the physical and the psychic. Thus, under the right conditions, atmospheric, personal, emotional, etc., an imprint is released. Some ghosts may be hallucinations of an imprint, and certain places can be hypothesised as being inherently more likely to have associated ghosts and hauntings, as well as certain times being peak times for this phenomenon to occur. Also certain people, those we call psychics or sensitives, are more likely to feel this energy imprint and respond to it by seeing or hearing the appropriate form or action. This is obviously only a part of the explanation, a spirit of a place or object is often far more than merely an imprint on a place with associated emotional, electrical, atmospheric charge.

Associated with the stone circles and other sacred sites are the so-called ley lines which also seem to be places of UFO sightings, hauntings, poltergeists and faery tales.

Ley Lines

Leys are essentially alignments of sacred sites, just as you get roads connecting villages, towns and cities. You can equate a major site with the energy of a city, while small local sites are like villages. The sacred site is the power place and the ley is the energy, or spirit, line linking it to the next site. It is ridiculous to talk about the power of a ley within a site like Avebury or Glastonbury – it is the whole site that is the power point. Most, if not all, stone circles have leys associated with them.

The best known of these, even called a Dragon Line by the National Trust, is the alignment that runs from St. Michael's Mount at Penzance in Cornwall up through Burrow Mump, Glastonbury Tor, Avebury and through to Bury St. Edmunds. It is aligned on the cross-quarter day sunrise and sunsets (of which more later), and this is what makes this place so magical. Nature has linked the movements of the sun with a series of very special hills that run all the way across England. No wonder the Celts found these places so special. If you stand on Glastonbury Tor, or Burrow Mump or the Cheesewring on Hallowe'en (Samhain), or Candlemas (Imbolc), you will see the sun set down the line. If you go to one of these places on May Day (Beltain), or Lammas (Lughnasadh), you will see the sun rise along the line. This is the power, the spirit, the energy of this very special Dragon line. I prefer to think of it in terms of the dragon, the earth energy, rather than the more modern Christian conception of St. Michael, because it is the earth's energy that I am celebrating, rather than that of the slayer of dragons.

Glastonbury also has an equinox line. Stand in the abbey and due west behind you is St. Benedict's church, whilst due east a foot path leads across Chalice Hill, down the back of the Tor and along a ridge of hills to finally end up at Stonehenge. So sunrise and sunset at Equinox link Glastonbury with Stonehenge.

Some people connect the ideas concerning ley lines with the Chinese belief in Feng-Shui, a divination system for landscaping, siting houses, roads, etc. which takes into account the chi energy of the land. And one can connect ley lines with the old Irish lore surrounding faery paths, on which one should never build a house, or obstruct in any way because to do so meant that bad luck would follow. I have seen a wonderful photo of a house in Ireland that has had the corner chopped off because it obstructed a faery path, and all manner of nasty poltergeist type things happened until it was rebuilt so as not to obstruct the path. If one understands ley lines as spirit paths along which the spirits fly, or energy paths along which psi energy flows then this tallies with such old lore. In other words as places where psychic experiences are more likely to happen.

Naturally if ancient sites are implicated in psychic events then so too are their associated leys. Devereux found that 37.5% of a random sample of leys showed evidence of UFO events occurring on them or in their immediate vicinity. I have personally witnessed a haunted house situated right on a leyline which has very strange effects on all living creatures who stay any length of time in the building and over which UFOs have been sighted. A map in Paul Devereux's book, *Earthlights*,[26] shows the strong correlation between UFOs, stone circles and ley lines: UFOs tend to be seen more often in geographical areas where there are stone circles or on the line between two sacred sites.

Many people feel that sacred sites, beacon hills, etc. are a sort of earth acupuncture point, a site of earth chi energy, and that ley lines are the meridian channels for this energy. This is an analogy that I have used for many years, because it seems intuitively to fit. Thus the ancient practice of lighting beacon fires on the beacon hills at midsummer and other sacred days is a bit like heat acupuncture of the earth's meridians. This analogy fits even better with the recent discovery that acupuncture points can be measured on our bodies using electrical skin resistance meters, the skin's electrical resistance at the acupuncture point differing from the area around. And with sacred sites, the GMF differs. This chi energy, whatever it is, not only links with geomagnetic energy but also with psychic energy, and it is a psychic force that we feel at stone circles and their associated leys. Paul Devereux[27] is at present exploring the idea that leys are spirit lines linked to shamanic flight paths when people used the sacred sites specifically to induce out-of-body journeys, which corroborates this idea.

Ley lines have a spiritual significance, in as much as there is a feel about them which lifts the spirits, which makes you gasp in wonder, which makes you feel good. They give you the feel that you could walk along them with seven league boots. Because presumably the Neolithic peoples were more in tune with the subtle GMF, and other earth energies of which we as yet know very little, because they did not have any form of electrical pollution, such as we labour under now in the form of electric pylons, power stations, roads, railways, television, radio waves, etc., almost *ad nauseam*, then they would be far more aware of the psychic potential of these places and appear to have had a science using this natural earth energy. I actually feel that many of the circles are places such as Doris Lessing[28] describes in *Shikasta*, places which are tuned in to stars for psychic communication, harmony of this planet's energies for evolutionary purposes. Stonehenge is a cosmic temple related to more than just movements of sun and moon; Callanish relates to the whole of the moon's cycle.

The Fair Folk and the Stones

Standing stones, stone circles, long barrows and cursuses – these monuments are all that is left of the Neolithic peoples of Britain and Europe who inhabited these Isles from the end of the Ice Age, about 9000 BC, until the coming of the Bronze Age Celts in about 2000 BC, who continued what the Neolithic had begun until the later invasion of Iron Age Celts about 500 BC. These Iron Age Celts are the people about whom the Celtic revival has focused: the Mabinogian,[29] Arthurian legends, runes, tree calendars, Druids, and so on are relics of ritual way of life of these people. In looking at the faery faith we look back to knowledge of a world-view before the Iron Age, before the Bronze Age to the Neolithic people, the megalith builders, the fair folk.

There is a wealth of legend around stone circles concerning visions and apparitions, lots of it linked to the Celtic faery faith. To me, the lore about faeries is our oral tradition about this earth magic, the peoples who built the megalithic monuments, identifying and enhancing the earth's energy at these points, and the ancient religion of these lands. If you read the lore and legends of Scotland, Ireland and Cornwall you will find numerous references to the fair folk living in tumuli and connected with the stone circles

Faery tales represent the degraded remnant of the old British animistic religion, now resurging as Wicca, or paganism, or natural magic, or the spiritual side of the Green movement. This faith, this philosophy, is the basis behind the newly evolving paganism in Britain, America, Australia and (to a lesser extent) Europe. Parapsychology, in giving us the scientific grounding for magic, is confirming this philosophy, is giving us a science of the spirit, so that we can grow a world-view in tune with our times that will be in harmony with what our planet needs for survival.

For me, my understanding of the pineal gland, its links with a psychic state of consciousness and with our sensitivity to the GMF enables us to earth our spirituality so that we can really start to understand and to live what we believe. We are being affected subliminally at all times by changes in the GMF and this has enormous implications for astrology, magic and witchcraft. May we all become far more sensitive, in tune and in harmony with this beautiful planet on which we have been born.

Evans Wentz says: 'Magic was the supreme science because it raised its adepts out of the ordinary level of humanity to a close relationship with the gods and creative powers. Nor was it a science to be had for the asking. Neophytes often spent twenty years in severe study and training. Most of the mysteries of antiquity were psychic or mystical in their nature'.[30]

Geopsychic magic – is that the reason for the megalithic monuments? The stone circles and the mounds, such as barrows and tumuli, are sacred sites at which space, time and mind are most effectively linked: the early working temples. The stone circles are perfectly designed to maximise active psi: visions, and healing type phenomena; the barrows are perfect for receptive psi, clairvoyance and divination. They are essentially absolutely practical, as well as sacred, in their function, places where the veils between this world of matter and the elusive world of spirit are thinnest – an elemental technology combining cosmic, atmospheric, geological and human factors.

The megaliths tell us that on this particular spot there is something special. The implications of this are enormous. They suggest that the Neolithic peoples who built these monuments were aware of the energy systems involved and manipulated them using critical times such as the solstices or full moons in order to enhance the geopsychic effects. This is a 'natural science' of which we have little knowledge at present, the interaction of our psyche with that of the planet, and hence with the rest of the solar system, and possibly even with the stars. The degraded relics of this science are present in our myths and folk-lores, and in some of the traditional occult systems, but they are no more than very degraded relics. In studying the stone circles I sense that an incredible wisdom existed in ancient times concerning the nature of our spiritual selves, and this wisdom is slowly but surely being distilled once again as we gain in knowledge and understanding and love of the stones and circles still standing.

2

Daemonic Reality:
Poltergeists and Piskies

Many poets, and all mystics and occult writers, in all ages and countries, have declared that behind the visible are chains on chains of conscious beings, who are not of heaven but of the earth, who have no inherent form, but change according to their whim, or the mind that sees them.

(Yeats, 1977)[1]

Poltergeists

Magic is the essence of faery. Psychic phenomena are the stuff of magic. There are hundreds of carefully proven cases of phenomena or apparitions precisely like many of those which people used to attribute to fair folk. These phenomena are, so to speak, the protoplasmic background of all religions, philosophies, or systems of mystical thought evolved on this planet. Faery phenomena are in one aspect essentially the same as 'spirit' phenomena, so the belief in fair folk ceases to be purely mythical, and faery visions are to be understood in psychic/spirit terms.

The following psychical phenomena have been linked with the fair folk: lots of people seeing an apparition at the same time, with very reliable witnesses; objects moving without contact; 'supernatural' raps and noises; telepathy; seership and visions; acquiring psychic knowledge in dream and trance states; mediumship or spirit possession.

Gervase[2] speaks of 'follets' who pelt the houses with stones, annoying people in much the same manner as was said of the brownies in Berwickshire, or the piskies in Cornwall. These were thought to be fairies who lived around the house and surrounding land, and who had been offended in some way and were wreaking revenge. This is a spirit interpretation of what is now called a poltergeist. According to Evans Wentz,[3] the fairies had an extraordinary zeal for neatness and decorum in all the circumstances of life. If everything in the house was not

Puck, the ultimate mischief maker. (Illustration courtesy of Brian Froud. Reproduced from Faeries *by Brian Froud and Alan Lee, Pan Books, 1979.)*

absolutely as it should be, the house cleaner was severely punished – pelting with stones, pinching, tormenting the person until they cleaned up. Nowadays most people tend to consider that poltergeist phenomena are related to a focus person who is deemed to be disturbed in some way. *Plus ça change.*

Poltergeist literally means 'noisy spirit' and is most commonly associated with the coarse and country faery who threshed the corn, churned the butter. One such being was called 'Lob-lie-by-the-fire' and he looked

36

'like a rough hurgin bear'. Puck is usually shaggy in appearance. The brownies of lowland Scotland and North England are dwarfish, rugged, doing odd jobs about farms and receiving milk and food. Hobgoblins, Robin Goodfellow – what names to conjure with. In Isle of Man fynodere another hairy sprite, in Ireland the leprechaun – like the English lubberkin. In Scotland the gruagach or hairy one looked after the cows, the urisk, the brollachan or fuath all rough and hairy (so reminiscent of Pan). All of these are associated with agriculture, a particular family and steading, and more particularly the household hearth.

Brownies were really quite touchy as is shown so well in the children's story 'The Elves and the Shoemaker' – if you get it wrong in some way then they won't help you any more. In the case of the elves and the shoemaker, it was the shoemaker saying thank you that caused the helpful elves to leave. Paradox is at the heart of faerie and of magic! In some parts of Scotland and Ireland there used to be a special stone outside the back door on which bread and milk would be put last thing at night as a thank you for the help received. There is a strong moral and ethical element in most faery tales.

Poltergeist phenomena are typical of faerie magic, because they are both substantially physical and yet at the same time when you go to investigate there is nothing there, and sceptics can easily convince themselves that it was all in the imagination. We have records of poltergeist phenomena since at least the 1600s. There are some cases where stones are thrown, some where pots and pans fly about the place, or furniture goes on fire. There are some where footsteps are heard on the stairs and door handles turn. The phenomena vary quite a lot from minor phenomena such as rappings heard around the house for a very short time to phenomena that can last for years, which may then be indistinguishable from a haunting. When the phenomenon is associated with a particular person, it is normally a young person in their teens or twenties. It usually occurs in the house where the person lives, but several cases have occurred where they work.

Most episodes involve movement of objects, which move in unusual trajectories. One rarely sees the object start moving – you only see it in flight or occasionally landing. Quite often it is extremely hot to touch, and often you will see it flying and then it will suddenly just drop to the floor. A large proportion of cases involve sound as well. Sometimes things go on fire as in the events in Italy in the 1980s where a Scottish nanny was taken to court for attempted murder, because the baby's cot caught fire. In this case some people viewed the phenomenon as witchcraft, implying that the girl was in some way consciously responsible, whereas in poltergeist phenomena it is generally considered that the phenomena are not being consciously caused – although often the children will play with them and throw stuff as well 'just for the hell of it'. Sometimes puddles of water appear and sometimes there are unusually hot or cold objects or areas of a room. There have even been cases of teleportation of objects.

What is striking about most of the phenomena is that they seem rather meaningless and rather like a mischievous boy playing games. Let's take the recent poltergeist case in Cardiff.[4] In an engineering workshop and retail shop in Cardiff during the early 1990s, carburettor floats were thrown, often impacting in the walls and ceilings. The people who worked there starting interacting and the phenomena then often occurred in response to someone asking the poltergeist to do something. Grass seed and fertiliser were scattered at night when the premises were locked, and once on the shoulders of a customer! Plates were smashed on the floor at night with the pieces lying arranged perfectly together instead of scattered apart. The engine from a commercial petrol mower was found running when the premises were opened on Monday morning – it could not have been left running over the weekend as it would have run out of petrol, so it must have been started some time before the shop was opened. It was the sort of mower that took three separate operations to start it, one of which was a powerful pull start. Cutlery was laid in place settings in the small kitchen table at the back of the premises. And, most kindly, there were regular appearances of money, totalling over 70, primarily in the form of rolled-up 5 notes pinned to the ceiling by carburettor floats, overnight while the premises were locked.

One of the people who worked there saw, on three occasions, an apparition of a small boy about 12 years old wearing short trousers and a peaked school cap, with no face visible under the cap and no outline of hands or bare knees, estimated to be two and a half feet tall. Now I ask you, have you ever seen a 12 year old boy who was two and a half feet tall! This sounds to me suspiciously like a sprite or brownie or mischievous piskie. The journal reports called it a 'responsive poltergeist' because he would throw things in response to requests, or money would appear when asked. Very childish in what occurred, no harm done to anyone and very shy of being seen.

Is this a poltergeist, is it a haunting, is it a brownie? Does it matter what we call it? The essential matter is that four adults running a very down to earth engineering workshop and shop experienced something that was very out of the ordinary that set them puzzling. They realised that life has more to it than the regular everyday working world. And one of them connected with a very mischievous spirit, whether apparition or faery it is difficult to say – certainly a wild and fun spirit. And that size is typical of beliefs about the fair folk – that they are different in size from us. So perhaps in a very ordinary place we have been touched by the supernatural, by the mystery, by the promise of something else.

Seances, Haunting and Apparitions of the Blessed Virgin Mary

We can recognise the same sort of phenomena in the mediumistic seances which were so popular during the Victorian era. In these seances there were odd noises such as music or voices, the table or objects moved about, raps were heard in the wood of the table, or from the walls or doors, floor, ceiling or table, occasionally there were disembodied voices, lights moving about, music heard, things floated about, apparitions formed, often only a hand which touched people, and so on. These were thought to be caused by spirits of the dead. In the heyday of mediums in Victorian times, some physical mediums used to have a semi-physical substance flowing out from their bodies, mouth or navel or vagina, which would then take on a form of a hand, or even a complete body of a person. This was called ectoplasm. Many photographs called 'spirit photographs' were taken of this weird, semi-physical stuff.

Evan Wentz notes that these are, in essence, as Flammarion says: '... really childish, puerile, vulgar, often ridiculous, and rather resemble the pranks of mischievous boys than serious bona-fide actions. It is impossible not to notice this. Why should the souls of the dead amuse themselves in this way? The supposition seems almost absurd'.[5]

Haunted houses show very similar sorts of phenomena to both poltergeist and mediumistic seances – sounds of footsteps, things getting moved, things appearing or disappearing, apparitions, voices, music, cold areas in the building, and so on. Normally haunting is thought to be related to the spirit of someone who once lived in the house. However, the traditional view of one type of ghost, the grey (or white) lady ghost, was that she was the faery spirit of the place, protecting the house, and that she would appear as a warning of some disaster about to happen. Forewarned is forearmed so, though she was feared, she played an important role. Traditionally she was called a banshee, which is Gaelic for faery (sidhe, pronounced shee) woman (ban), and people often described the banshee by the eerie sound that she made, either weeping and wailing or, less commonly, music. I have a piece of music, heard in Yorkshire on the moors, said to have been made by a banshee, which is identical with music heard on the Isle of Lewis, the northernmost isle in the Outer Hebrides.

A traditional depiction of a grey lady ghost, this one actually known as the brown lady of Raynham Hall. (Photograph taken by Indra Shira and first published in Country Life in 1936. Illustration courtesy of Mary Evans Picture Library.)

Reports of crisis, or bereavement apparitions are also very similar to traditions about faery apparitions giving news of death. In a crisis apparition you see someone and then discover either that they have just died or they are warning you that someone is in need of help. This is one of the most commonly reported forms of apparition and often occurs about 3 a.m., the person being woken from sleep and the apparition either smiling at the person and then leaving, or saying

The one and only photograph supposedly of an out-of-body person (Mme. Lambert) in existence. This was taken by Carrington, who was one of the first researchers into OBEs. (Reproduced from Modern Psychical Phenomena *by H. Carrington, Dodd, Mead & Co., 1919, p. 146.)*

something – like 'Good-bye'. The apparition may appear as if life like, or may be rather ethereal, with a sort of light about them. It is this second type that is closest to the grey lady ghost banshee – and is the traditional form. People who claim to be able to see someone who is out-of-body also depict an apparition that is almost identical to that of a grey lady. So it seems as if the apparition, whether of a ghost, someone out-of-body, or what used to be called a banshee, often take the same form, normally a silvery light white robed figure, and of course sometimes life-like.

    This, whatever it is that leaves the body when one has an out-of-body experience, can be a purely mental experience or can be a form of energy, which can be 'seen' by psychics, of which animals appear to be aware, that has perhaps been photographed. Two experiments in para-psychology explored this, whatever it is that appears to leave the body. In

The BVM apparition at Zeitoun in Cairo. The similarity between this apparition, the grey lady ghost, and the OBE apparition depicted by Carrington, is remarkable. (Reproduced from The Evidence for Visions of the Virgin Mary *by K. McClure, Aquarian Press, 1983.)*

one experiment, Keith Harary[6] reported leaving his body and going to his two kittens who were in a room with a one way screen through which they were being videotaped and recorded. At those times when Harary said he was visiting the kittens they moved about less and went to the area of the room he reported visiting. This suggests that a 'psychic detector' can become aware of whatever it is that leaves the body.

In another experiment, Alex Tanous[7] had to describe an optical target that could only be viewed at a particular place. At that place were strain gauges, crystals which respond to pressure – the piezoelectric effect mentioned in the previous chapter. These had been found in spoon bending experiments with children to respond to psychic 'force' when the spoon was not being touched. These strain gauges recorded something on those occasions when Tanous reported the target correctly, suggesting that whatever it is that leaves the body can exert a psychokinetic force.

It shows up as light – a light body, an energy body, being enlightened?! It is an electrical halfway house between the physical and the

The Lady of the Lake – a traditional faery water spirit, once again showing the same form as the previous three photographs. (Illustration courtesy of Alan Lee. Reproduced from Faeries *by Brian Froud and Alan Lee, Pan Books, 1979.)*

psychic. It is perhaps a mental energy, perhaps emotional energy. We don't know. It is perhaps the same psychic-physical substance as Kirlian photography, which shows up the electrical energy around the body, what is called corona discharge, a bit like the corona around the sun. Maybe this is the stuff of ectoplasm from physical mediums which was reported more commonly in Victorian times and which formed into hands, or heads or even complete bodies in the séance rooms. Perhaps it is the same energy as white lady ghosts, the light seen as a vision of the Blessed Virgin Mary (BVM), and of apparitions of the spirit of someone who has died. It is the energy of what Patrick Harpur[8] calls 'The Daimonic Reality', the reality which has one foot in the material world and one foot in the world of psyche, of spirit.

This energy can sometimes be linked with the earth's energy, with the GMF, as was talked about in the first chapter. Persinger[9] has noticed a relationship between a BVM episode and a geological fault. This remarkable case occurred at Zeitoun in Cairo in the 1960s, where thousands of people saw a bright light over a Coptic Christian church for a period of several weeks. Many of them saw a figure within the light and called it the Blessed Virgin Mary. Shortly after the visions ceased there was an earthquake a few hundred miles south of Cairo. This suggests that the anomalous magnetic field, due to the pressure rising in the rocks with the upcoming tremor, was linked with a vision seen by thousands. It also suggests that in an area of powerful earth energy we are affected psychically so that we are more likely to perceive apparitions, experience poltergeist phenomena or haunting.

There are many points of correspondence between BVM apparitions and fairies[10]: a strange glove of light of varying intensity; luminous entities within or close to this light; absence of rain at the site of the apparition, even though it is raining all around; miraculous cures; sweet music often announcing the figure and, especially with fairies, the playing of the most exquisite music the person has ever heard; flowers growing out of season — the faery otherworld is a place of perpetual summer; a sign given to the human messenger of apparent worthlessness turning out to be a miracle, as in the BVM of Guadeloupe in Mexico.

And so we see that hauntings, mediumistic séances, apparitions, poltergeists and faery activity all show the same type of phenomena.

Crop Circles and Circle Dancing

Many people nowadays consider that all the corn circles are made by human artists, and they are certainly very beautiful artwork. There are some who still feel that they have otherworldly origins. I am not here concerned with this debate about by whom and how they are made. I am concerned only about the effect they have on us and their mythological import, as a typical example of the poltergeistery, mischievous type of phenomena associated with the fair folk. Corn circles can be seen to be a form of this new–old phenomenon, that was previously attributed to the fair folk, as witnessed in a poem that Geoffrey Ashe mentions in his section on the fair folk in his book *Mythology of the British Isles*.[11] It is by Richard Corbet (1582–1635) and entitled: 'Farewell, rewards and fairies':

> Witness those rings and roundelays
> Of theirs, which yet remain,
> Were footed in Queen Mary's days
> On many a grassy plain;
> But since of late Elizabeth
> And later James came in,
> They never danced on any heath
> As when the time hath been.
>
> By which we note that fairies
> Were of the old profession;
> Their songs were Ave-Maries,
> Their dances were procession.
> But now, alas, they all are dead;
> Or gone beyond the seas;
> Or farther for religion fled,
> Or else they take their ease.

I find this poem very interesting, because he marks the time of the passing of the fairies as that of the witch hunts when the pagan people of Britain were finally driven completely underground by the Puritan Christian church. The time of Elizabeth I and James VI of Scotland (later James I of England) were at the peak of the witch trials; and the curious reference to the old profession makes me suspect that he refers to magical ability, called the Craft in humans, and to the worship of the goddess who was by this time depicted mainly as the Virgin Mary and loved by Roman Catholics though the Puritans removed her from their churches (Ave Marias were their songs).

When I was a child, faery rings were linked with mushroom circles. This is interesting because of the link between fairies and hallucinogenic mushrooms, such as *Psilocybin* and *Amanita muscaria*. This is a similar link as that mentioned with the shamanic usage of ayahuasca, psychotropic plants take us into another reality. But it does not explain the poem's lament that the fairies are no longer dancing their rings and roundelays, for the mushroom rings did not cease at the time of Elizabeth and James,

The Mowing - Devil :

Or, Strange *NEWS* out of

Hartford - fhire.

Being a True Relation of a Farmer, who Bargaining
with a Poor *Mower*, about the Cutting down Three Half
Acres of *Oats*; upon the *Mower's* asking too much, the *Farmer* fwore, *That the Devil fhould Mow it, rather than He.*
And fo it fell out, that that very Night, the Crop of *Oats*
fhew'd as if it had been. all of a Flame; but next Morning
appear'd fo neatly Mow'd by the Devil, or fome Infernal Spirit, that no Mortal Man was able to do the like.
Alfo, How the faid *Oats* ly now in the Field, and the Owner
has not Power to fetch them away.

Licenfed, *Auguft* 22th, 1678.

*The devil mowing; thought by many to be the first illustration of a crop circle, from 1678.
(Reproduced from Reproduced from* Fortean Times, *R.J. Rickard and P. Sieveking
(eds.), 1989, 53, p.38.)*

whereas perhaps the corn circle equivalent of that time did cease. There is
a woodcut from the same time, 1678, about a mowing devil, which some
consider to be a corn circle from that time, clearly linked with the devil,
which takes us back to the link between witches and fairies and corn

A traditional depiction of fairies dancing in a circle by a stone circle. ("And The Fairies danced in the mist" illustration courtesy of Monica Sjöö.)

circles, since at that time witchcraft and the fair folk were connected the devil.[12] And now with the corn circles it seems as though, at a mythological level, at a faery story type of reality, they are dancing their rings and roundelays yet again.

I have also noticed that, when first reported in the early 1980s, the rings were single large rings, and that since then they have increased not only in number but in complexity of pattern. Whatever is causing these rings, whether human jokers or something else, has a sense of humour, for no sooner have the researchers decided that they have understood how the rings are formed and have defined the limits on their formation, than rings have appeared which defy these limits. This has a very pixieish quality to it.

Another link I make between corn circles and fair folk, is the ancient practice of circle dancing within the stone circles. This dancing would have been circle dancing as in the national Breton rondo or ride, at stone circles which, like the dance, are circular in form. It is thought that these circle dances are memories of ancient initiation dances; they are definitely highly spiritual dances, related to both sun and moon. To dance these dances in the stone circles is strong magic for invoking spirits such as the fair folk represent.

This circular initiation dance has come to be attributed to corrigans in Brittany, to pixies in Cornwall and England, and to the fair folk in these and other Celtic countries. Circle dances, like the Breton ones, used to take place at weddings in the Channel Islands, the revolution being around a person not a stone, and the people bowed to this central person. Evans Wentz[13] notes that if the dance was pictured as a circle with a dot in the centre, we have the astronomical symbol still used by astrologers to represent the sun. He says that in Guernsey the sites of principal dolmens or standing stones 'were visited in sacred procession, and round certain of them the whole body of pilgrims solemnly revolved three times from east to west'. And fairies were considered the best musicians, and to visit faeryland and be taught to play, was held to be the highest possible musical gift one could acquire.

Several of the stone circles have tales linking them with faery musicians. Evans Wentz also notes that the place for holding a gorsedd (a sort of modern Welsh initiation), under the authority of which the Eisteddfod (an annual Welsh festival of song, poetry and dance) is conducted, was also within a circle of stones, face to face with the sun as there was no power to hold a gorsedd under cover or at night, but only where and as long as the sun was visible.

Have you noticed the synchronicity between the recent trend of circle dancing and the reappearance of corn circles? Circle dancing is universal and is still practised by, for example, some Amerindian peoples, and is once more becoming increasingly popular. It hits a chord within people at this time and so feels good to do, particularly when performing ceremony. As far as I can tell the craze for circle dancing started about 1980, after it was introduced to the Findhorn community in Scotland. The first circles to be reported in a newspaper were in 1980. I wonder if there is some sort of a link, other than the synchronistic one. Circle dancing seems to be the most ancient form of dance that we know of. My suggestion here is that the dancing in circles being done by so many thousands of people now all over the country is a sort of sympathetic magic which is recharging the earth so that phenomena connected with spirits of the earth are reappearing.

The thing I really love about corn circles is that up until the 1900s everyone in the village would go out to the fields at Lammastide – when the corn was being cut to help with the harvest. There was quite a party atmosphere for all that it was very hard work. Nowadays there is one man in a combine harvester. The fields are dead. And then corn circles appear and once again there are hundreds, even thousands of people in the corn fields, having a picnic, dancing in circles, singing, doing ritual and just generally having fun or wandering through the fields. Once more there is life in the fields at harvest time. Magically this is wonderful. May it continue!

The Daemonic Reality

Daemonic phenomena[14] are those phenomena that are part physical, part psychic and part mythic. They contain all the elements of a myth that can serve various purposes, seeing an apparition (ghost or mediumistic spirit) could be comforting to a recently bereaved person; seeing the BVM gives religious inspiration. Seeing a faery supports a world-view, a philosophy, a belief in the otherworld, in spirit immanent in nature. The daemonic are like mortals, but not mortal, to the *objective* world are non-existent, yet to the *subjective* world are fully living and conscious.

The daemonic is linked to our world but is not of this world. This is illustrated by the curious link between the person's experience with them and the progress of human technology, the daemonic always being different in their technology from us. They are either more advanced than us in some way, as in their ability to appear and disappear, or less advanced, as in their medical technology. For example, the fair folk always seem to dress and have a culture of a time earlier than ours, and their 'superiority' lies solely in their magical abilities.

Our connection with the daemonic reality is in part fed by our imagination. Imagination is the supreme art of the human mind. It is our imagination that gives us our music, our fine art, our architecture, our literature, plays, poetry, our civilisation. And yet what is this property, the imagination, the key aspect of our human psyche? To denigrate the imagination is to denigrate that which makes us human, that aspect of the mind which is unique to our species, our creativity in which we dare to behave like the gods. Somewhere I read that the derivation of the word 'magic' is from the Chaldean 'Magdhim', the meaning of which is wisdom, allied with the qualities summed up in the term philosophy. From this root the words image and imagination are also derived. I make this brief allusion to root words because I feel we can learn so much about a topic from its word derivation. Imagine comes from the root 'magi', which we know, from our Christmas mythology, means the 'wise men', who came to visit the baby Jesus; so our imagination is linked with wisdom. I like to think of magicians as people who are travelling the path of wisdom, attempting to become wise men and women, or cunning men in the old British terminology. In Terry Pratchett's[15] words, they are practitioners of 'headology'. So there is a turn around for you – next time you say 'just my imagination' think of what you are really saying.

We live in a material culture. We think that the REAL world is the physical. We say: 'Just your imagination'. I say that the world of mind, of spirit, of the imagination, is as real as the physical. This is the foundation stone of the faery faith – the knowledge that we live in our minds as much as, if not more than, we live in our bodies, and that this is as real as any other aspect of our life — the knowledge that the mind shapes our reality all the time.

The human imagination is the creative aspect of the mind, and magic uses the mind in a particular way in which the imagination creates directly. Alexandra David-Neel[16] tells a story of creating a tulpa when living in Tibet. A tulpa is a human created through the use of imagination; at first you visualise it in your mind's eye, and over the weeks and months of visualising it so it becomes sort of ghostlike, and then other people can sense it. In her story, the tulpa she created of a Tibetan monk became so solid and real that it started doing things of its own accord and became a huge problem for her — so she then had to dissolve it, which took even more effort than creating it. I was told a similar tale in my parapsychology class in 2000. The person's daughter had an imaginary friend. One evening she took a photo of her daughter sleeping, and when the photo was developed there was another child asleep in the bed with her daughter, whom her daughter identified as her imaginary friend. Is this her imaginary friend revealed on a photo as ghosts sometimes are? It looks just like an ordinary child. We only have the experience of the mother and her daughter. There is no other validating testimony that we can rely on. And so, as always, it comes down to trust, to faith, to belief, another foundation stone of the faery faith.

Understanding illusion and the part it plays in the development of understanding is an important part of the faery faith. The function of illusion in magic is to create an atmosphere. The purpose of this atmosphere is to condition the mind by the seemingly miraculous to the reality of phenomena which also appear miraculous, because not subject to physical laws. I think that in the original shamanic arts, stage conjuring and true magic went hand in hand. Under the pretence and behind the mask, reality is there. Parapsychological research has recently come to endorse this view, especially in the work of Batcheldor,[17] who was investigating table tipping in seances. He found that if in the course of the evening somebody deliberately nudged the table, so that everyone in the room went 'Oh the table just moved', this would help the psychic effect of the table moving through psychokinesis to occur. Once everyone in the room believes that magic is happening, then it can happen. It's all in the mind!

And this is the place of the mischievous tricksy pisky.

Illusion feeds imagination, and disciplined imagination is necessary to the opening up of new stages and degrees of experience. The operative word here is discipline. Imagination and illusion are tools, not ends in themselves. Imagination must be controlled, illusion must be recognised.

Perhaps the reason why so many parapsychologists have had difficulty in obtaining clear and strong results in their experiments is that they have not used participants who have had the necessary training in this disciplined use of the imagination. The basic idea behind these methods is that out-picturing sets in motion a force which brings what is imagined, or imagined intensely, into manifestation – perhaps not immediately but,if you keep on working at it, in time you will create that which you wish.

Powerful aids to the building of illusion, or inducing change in consciousness, are rhythm; vibration as used in drumming, but also as used in poetry and song. Perhaps this is the reason poetry, chanting and song have always been associated with rituals and magic. Poetry has been called 'the language of the subconscious', possibly because the subconscious appears to more easily accept suggestions given to it in rhythmic form. Poetry is the natural language of faery, which has always used it, not only in spell-making but also to convey its wisdom and mysteries.

Our mythology is our creative imagination related to our conceptions of divinity. We create our gods, as Pratchett so wonderfully describes in 'Small Gods'.[18] Our gods depend on us to believe in them and if we don't they fade away, or, as Douglas Adams describes in 'The Long Dark Tea Time of the Soul',[19] they change character totally.

Go into a megalithic site; what were the gods of these people? This is the age of Cernunnos maybe, except that Cernunnos as we understand him is a later Bronze Age form, but he has a resemblance to the horned shaman in the Cave des Trois Frères. We no longer even know the names of the old gods of the Palaeolithic time – they have faded even from our memory. But perhaps in the faery stories we can once again connect with their energy, for I feel that the old tales of these isles are the remnants of an oral, bardic tradition that stretches 6000–10,000 years. Look at the power of our myths, they rule our culture, which rules the way we think, feel and behave. This is easier done by looking at cultures other than our own, say American Indian shamanic culture or the Moslem culture, if one is living in a Christian culture. And remember that the culture you are living in, with its mythology and beliefs, is forming the whole of your being. It is only by getting a perspective on it by living within another culture that you can see what it is doing to you. It is only when the fish is out of water that it knows what water is!

As Jacques Vallée says so eloquently: 'Mythology rules at a level of our social reality over which normal political and intellectual trends have no real power – time frames are long and evolution is slow. But these long term changes dominate the destiny of civilisations. Myths

This Paleolithic cave painting of a dancing shaman from 35,000 years ago shows how ancient and deep rooted the magical belief system is.

define the set of things one can think about. They operate via symbols – a metalogical system. It violates no laws because it is the substance of which laws are made'.[20]

The mythic reality is part of the collective unconscious, as Jung called it. This is an aspect of mind which thinks symbolically, and particularly that aspect in which the archetypes are to be found. This is the realm of primary process thought as psychologists call it, the type of thinking that very young children use, which is why they love faery stories so much because they relate to that magical, symbolic, archetypal form of tale. Our dream mind links with the collective unconscious when we experience big dreams: those dreams which occur now and then, which are not the normal kitchen sink type of dream, which is processing yesterday and tomorrow and all the stuff which has come in; nor is it the type of dream which is dealing with all of our unconscious stuff from childhood, our personal psychotherapy; but the sort of dream in which we connect with divinity, with spirit, with archetype.

A good example is one in which I was standing on a cliff top with this older woman on my left. She occurs in my dreams at significant times and I think of her as my inner guide. She is the archetypal wise old woman. We saw an eagle flying and it swooped and caught a rainbow dove in its talons, and we could see the back being broken and the blood dripping from the talons. It flew over to where we were standing and landed and offered the dove to me. I was so honoured, so over-whelmed that I bowed right down to the ground in the yogic embryo pose, so that I was curled up in foetal position on my legs with my whole body and head to the ground and my arms folded back to my feet. The next thing I knew was that the eagle had picked me up in its talons. I could feel the leathery texture around my back, but it was gentle, not hurting me, though the talons were strong, and it carried me and I flew with it. I shall never forget this dream. As I write it, it is as vivid as when I experienced it.

This is the level of mind that our greatest art, scientific discovery, music come from – the sort of dream that Elias Howe had when he realised how to devise a needle with the hole in the tip so a sewing machine could work. He had a nightmare, in which he had been captured by cannibals who were about to cook him, and he saw that they had spears with holes in the tip of the spear, the whole of human experience of sewing from Mesolithic times. This level of creativity, overcoming ten thousand years of using needles with holes at the back end, is the sort of dream where we walk with the gods, the sort of dream that has the same power as a vision of the BVM, or seeing a ghost, or a UFO. This level of the creative mind is awesome. If you can conceive of something, then it can manifest into physical reality and into your life, but the mental conception comes first. This is the level of reality that we are dealing with, the daemonic reality, what I call psychic reality, because this is the level of mind that shamans use when they go out of body, travel with their spirit guide for the purpose of clairvoyance, precognition, healing or getting wise counsel to some problem that the tribe need answering – the level of mind we use when we connect with faery. To connect with faery you must shift into primary process, archetypal, daemonic mind.

The Physics of Psyche

Fairies are a psychic reality through which an alien form of intelligence, a daemonic intelligence, archetypal consciousness, is communicating with us. They are alien because they are not human, their way of thinking is not human, their concerns are not human, any more than a tree's or a mountain's consciousness or concerns are human. The consciousness of Gaia, our planet Earth, is not a human consciousness. For example, the time span is not human and so is utterly alien to us. Just as we say that one of our years is like seven years to a dog or a cat, so, at least in the Celtic mythology, with the fair folk one of our years is like a night and a day to them (In Celtic reckoning the day starts at sunset hence the night comes first.) Just think for a moment on that perspective, and the otherworld nature of it. This shift of time and space is an interesting one. One of our days is like one of their years. If you live for one year in faeryland that is 365 years on this earth. If an elf were to live to be 100 years old, that would be 36,500 of our years – right back to the Palaeolithic in fact, in one lifetime. This is not divinity, in that the divine is immortal – there is no time – all is now, but it is very close to divinity in that time is much slower than for us. No wonder their concerns are other than ours. Just as for a gnat, time is much faster because they only live for three of our days, so for them one of our days is like 30 years. To a gnat we are immortal. And so to the faery we are as gnats. In their perspective, here today gone tomorrow. Never forget this! The philosophy that arises from this has links with modern science, such as relativity of time. And so the legends take on another dimension – that of Einstein and modern physics!

In Einstein's Relativity Theory, at the speed of light time stands still. And at the speed of light matter becomes infinite mass. Is this what is meant to be enlightened? Or in your light body? For there to be no movement in time. This is immortality, this is divinity when it is always now, when time does not move. And at the speed of light, time is always now. Light in itself does not experience time; when it leaves the star and when it arrives at your eye so you can see the star, for that photon, that wave, of light there has been no movement in time, it is the same time as it was when it left the star. As the mystic, William Blake wrote:

> 'To see the universe in a grain of sand,
> Heaven in a wild flower;
> To hold infinity in the palm of your hand
> And eternity in an hour'.[21]

Time is relative. Our current concepts about space and time need changing more in line with Einstein's ideas; the relativity of time is totally appropriate when dealing with these realms. This is best understood from the classic example of a pair of twins living on Earth, and one of them going off on a rocket at nearly the speed of light for what seems to the one on Earth to be 20 years. But, because time is related to speed, for the one on the rocket it is only two years, so when they return their twin who stayed on Earth is 18 years older than them.

The speed of light is said to be 186,000 miles per second. A friend of mine looking at these ideas about this Rip van Winkle effect connected with faery (or that wonderful book *The King of Elfland's Daughter*[22]), worked out the speed of sprite to be something like 143,000 miles per second. Nearly the speed of light, but not quite. To me this is the essence of that reality we call faery, and also of their craft we call magic. In faeryland one is not at the speed of light because time does pass, but much more slowly than here, so one is in a frequency domain that is part way towards the eternal timeless realm.

And so we can see that a larger reality, other dimensions, exist. Energy and information are related. Let me talk briefly about a physics of information – the relationship between psyche and matter. These ideas come from work initiated by David Bohm,[23] and are often called the Holographic Paradigm (Wilber[24]) or Holographic Universe (as in my book, or the one by Talbot,[25] which synchronistically was published the same year as my book using the same title, mine for one of my chapters, his for the whole book). Lots of people now have written about these so-called 'quantum' ideas on how to understand certain aspects of the universe in which we live, and so far these make the most sense to me of the physics of the psyche.

Since the time of Einstein, most physicists have come to understand that all energy is matter, and vice versa. An electron can be seen as a material particle or as an energy wave. The same with light which we normally think of as an energy wave, and which is also a matter particle, the photon. Thus everything is both matter and energy all the time – the form in which we detect it depends on the detector. This has led to theories which say that the act of observation is one of the key factors in what actually happens.

Consciousness plays an active role in whether the electron or photon (light) manifests as a particle or wave, which is called 'collapsing the wave function'. This is the so-called Schrödinger cat paradox, in which you imagine a box with a cat in it. There is a random element in the box, which will trigger a cyanide capsule, but because it is totally random, until you look you don't know whether or not the cat is dead. At the quantum level a substance is everything it can possibly be, until fixed by observation, so the random element both has and has not occurred, the capsule both has and has not been broken, the cat is both alive and dead at the same time. Until the box is opened and someone looks in, anything and everything is true all at once. This idea has been explored in depth by a physicist, who is also a parapsychologist, called Schmidt,[26] and his results do indeed suggest that it is the mind of the observer who determines the reality that occurs. His results have been replicated at Princeton by the Princeton Engineering Anomalies Research (PEAR) laboratory,[27] and they have found that a random element can show non-random discharge depending on what the observer wishes. Say you want it to discharge more than normal, then this is what you get; or less than normal, this is what you get. So the mind, will, consciousness, or intent of the observer affects what actually manifests. Therefore, Bohm[28] suggests that we have not just a matter–energy link as in Einstein's equation, but a three-way triangle: energy–matter–mind, or information, consciousness or meaning, as different people prefer to label this aspect. Mind interacts with energy and with matter to create the reality in which we exist. This suggests that if you want the cat to live, then there is a good chance that the cat will be alive when you open the box – consciousness interferes with randomicity.

The old paradox of whether or not a tree makes a noise when it falls in the forest without someone there to witness it, is resolved by considering that at one level everything has a consciousness of sorts – even the universe. These ideas also suggest that at one level everything is interconnected. In physics this is called the EPR paradox, or Bell's theorem. Nowadays this is called quantum entanglement. This experiment measures two photons of light that have come from one thing and so are interconnected, or entangled, in which case one spins one way and the other balances it out completely by spinning in the opposite way. If one of these photons is then interfered with so that its spin is altered, the other will alter its spin to compensate, so as to maintain the equal and opposite polarity. In Bell's Theorem, once two photons have been together, then anything that subsequently happens to one will affect the other however far apart they are in space and time. There can be no material or energy thing passing between the two of them, yet the information about the change in spin is transmitted from one to the other. When translated into metaphysics, this experiment says that information about the state of one thing is intimately interconnected to the state of whatever was initially part of the same system. The two are at one level, indivisible and linked by information, by meaning, at all times. If we accept the current myth about the beginning of the universe, the Big Bang Myth, then this says that in the beginning it was all one (which is what is meant by the term 'singularity'), and so everything in the whole universe is intimately interconnected to everything else, and Blake's vision comes into force. Anything that happens anywhere affects everything else, so as to maintain the balance. Thus we live in an interconnected world.

Thus there is no problem at this level of whether or not ghosts, fairies, BVM apparitions are physical or not, because within the new quantum concept they are both physical and psychic at one and the same time, just as in poltergeist or haunting phenomena where the physical action, such as the door opening by itself, is undeniable and yet the causal force is psychic. We can understand the physical world as a universe of information events. This means that consciousness is not simply a local function of the human brain but is immanent throughout the universe, and there is a sort of consciousness within a photon. This is the sort of consciousness that responds appropriately when its partner photon is altered. Many parapsychologists are taking these findings from quantum physics and using them to create a theory about paranormal phenomena.

The age-old philosophies of 'humans being a microcosm of the macrocosm' and 'as above so below' are now being propounded through the new physics, which has become metaphysical, which I find immensely amusing and great fun. I consider it is the modern version of the worm Ouroborus – in physics we have studied matter right to the end of the tail, and it has turned into spirit.

The reason I call it the Holographic Universe is that a hologram is a picture made from light waves interfering with one another. This light substance is a fascinating medium because it does not work like familiar matter. Light is a quantum phenomenon – it can be a particle (a photon) or it can be a wave. Whether it is one or the other depends on how you choose to measure it. Until it is measured, i.e. interacts with matter, it is in both possibilities at the same time. When we capture it in a photograph we materialise it as a physical substance. If you tear a photograph in half you get two halves which are different, but if you capture it as a hologram you materialise it in its wave form. If broken in half it forms two whole pictures, as seen from the perspective of each half. If broken into four, you get four whole pictures as seen from the perspective of each quarter, and if you cut a hologram into 400,000 pieces you get 400,000 whole pictures, albeit from the perspective of each part. In other words, each part contains the whole, and the whole is in each part. Thus every bit of the hologram contains the whole as seen from the perspective of that bit. As with Bell's theorem this metaphor can be expanded to the whole universe. Therefore, I am the whole universe from the perspective of Serena, and you are the whole universe from your perspective. The whole is contained in every part, and as it was all one at the beginning, so at this level there is no here and there, no now and then, it is all one, all now. Thus in clairvoyance, there is no distance between oneself and the information – at one level you are one with all information. There is no time either, so you can know the future – or at least a highly probable item.

This level of being is a probabilistic universe. Which means that everything is possible, as described so wonderfully by Douglas Adams[29] in *The Hitchhiker's Guide to the Universe*, in which the space ship, the 'Heart of Gold', is powered by quantum paradox in which anything can happen (and does), it is just that some things are more probable than others.

In Conclusion

We seem to need contact with this daemonic reality, throughout most cultures throughout most of human history, with ghosts, apparitions and the fair folk; in the Victorian era through table turning, planchettes and mediums; in our technological era through BVM apparitions, poltergeists and UFO space beings. As we have seen in parapsychology it is the artists, musicians, actors who are most able to score successfully on psi tests – to go into altered states of consciousness and have visions. And children the world over see fairies. These are the people who are still aware and alive to the numinous in nature around, who see these things – not the academic or the scientist, or the city dweller whose mind has become hard through left-brain training and work. We do not have shamanic experiences so readily because our minds are too strong, our literate civilisation has trained our left-brain verbal mind and the faery or UFO experience is a right-brain non-verbal experience.

And so we enter the realm of faery – through magic, through our experience of psychic phenomena. Throughout all cultures and all times people have had these experiences. People are still having these experiences. Lots. We are calling them by another name but it is just the most recent form of the Daemonic Reality – for if you shut one opening another will form. We used to connect with the beings of the earth Recently we have called them poltergeists, or grey lady ghosts, not recognising their faery nature. Nowadays we are connecting with beings of the air. The form of the beings is the same as of old but they are not being recognised because no-one remembers what the fair folk used to look like. Nowadays they are being called greys, and are thought to come from space, because nowadays our culture is looking to the heavens in order to escape from the problems we have created on this earth – and this is where we are meeting our divine ones and our demons.

3

UFOs: The Airy-Fairy
Lore of Today

*We are living in the early years of a new mythological movement,
giving our technological age its faeryland. Because UFOs appear
scientific and self-consistent and yet irreconcilable with our present
day scientific knowledge a logical vacuum is created that the human
imagination tries to fill. Such situations give us the highest and the
basest forms of religious, poetic and political activity.*

(Vallée, 1970)[1]

Have We as a Western Culture Created the Aliens of UFO Lore?

Nowadays, the sorts of phenomena that I have been talking about in the previous two chapters are more likely to be connected with UFOs than faeries. This perspective is in essence what I call the European hypothesis, and it has been proposed first by Carl Jung[2], more recently by Jacques Vallée,[3] Hilary Evans[4] and also Paul Devereux in his *Earthlights*[5] hypothesis.

Modern day UFO phenomena bear a striking resemblance to faery folklore in varying ways. The points of correspondence between the various otherworld beings who we keep on interacting with throughout the ages and throughout all parts of the world, are so numerous that, once we have been shown them, we cannot fail to recognise them in whatever disguise they may show themselves.

First, the physical: the shape of the typical circular UFO craft is very similar to that of a circular mound, commonly known as tumulus, or rath, or fort, lifted off the ground with the ring of bright light, the lit window of the craft being equivalent to the light from the hall in which the fair folk are dancing.

The size and shape of the various UFO occupants is very similar to that of the legends of the different races of fair folk; either tall and fine

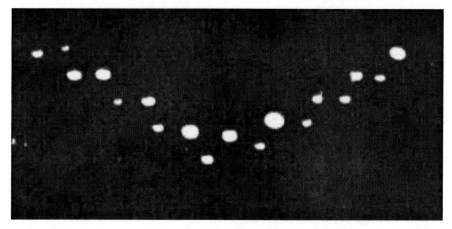

Most UFOs are seen as lights in the sky. This photograph of what came to be called "The Lubbock Lights" was taken by Carl Hunt in Texas, August 1952. (Illustration reproduced from www.subversiveelement.com/lubbocklights)

Artist's impression of a landing in a lavender field in France, July 1965. Though the picture is a fake as you get them, it illustrates the point that the form of both vehicle and occupants is similar to traditional depictions of faeries in their raths, of which we also only have artists' illustrations. (Illustration courtesy of Mary Evans Picture Library.)

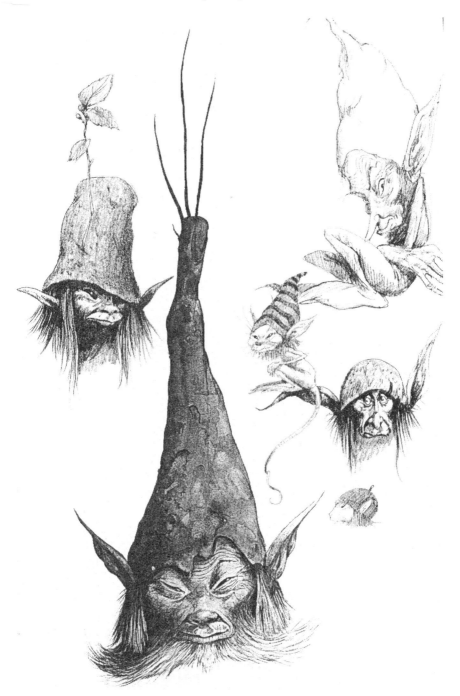

(a) Pixies (Illustration courtesy of Brian Froud. Reproduced from Faeries *by Brian Froud and Alan Lee, Pan Books, 1979)*

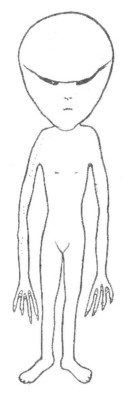
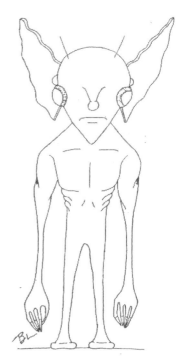

(b) Two modern representations of UFO beings. Notice the similarity with those of traditional pixies. (Illustration reproduced from Mysteries of the Unknown: The UFO Phenomenon, *Time-Life Books, 1987.)*

featured, wearing silvery light clothing; or they are small and misshapen with large heads and big eyes. Hilary Evans[6] in his book about UFOs has percentages which show that the number of times the greys are seen is equivalent to the number of reports of pixie type beings, and the number of times silver space-suited type beings are encountered is equivalent to sightings of the shining ones, or grey lady type beings: 20% humanoid; 34% bipeds with large heads; 5% hairy bipeds; 30% silver space suits.

Both faery and UFO beings are alien to us. Their concerns are not ours and yet they interact with us. It seems that we always have something that they want, a life force that they need, and so we have stories of changelings, or abductions and implants. Abduction stories are very similar in feel with the changeling tales. The primary difference is that faeries are beings of the earth and UFO aliens are beings of space – of the air.

The first connection I had with this sort of energy was when I first moved to Glastonbury, and walking to the pub one night I saw a huge flash of light around the back of Chalice Hill over towards the Tor. I stopped and there was another one. This went on for some minutes and finally I went on my way, not sure what it was I had experienced – no explanation in my mind either then or now. A year or two later I had the same experience but with sound. Last thing at night, whilst I was putting the milk bottles out on the front doorstep, there was this strange, high-pitched humming sound in the sky across the road from my house. I heard this sound on several occasions and my neighbour also heard it. She then had a visitation from a space being, silver-suited, human size, who sat in her living room and conversed with her. These sounds went on for some months, but I never met any beings! Then when bicycling up the hill one day, I looked out over the levels which stretch for forty miles all the way to the Bristol Channel and over to Wales. I saw an object flying in the sky about twenty miles away. What caught my attention was that it would fly in a straight line and then sharply change direction. I watched it for about ten minutes, and then it disappeared behind a cloud and never reappeared. And my final experience was when I was washing up looking out the window. Some low flying jets roared past below the level of my house; I was looking down on them. And whilst their noise was still rending the air, flying in the opposite direction, totally silently, came a silver cigar shaped object, going just as fast, but definitely not with the same violence. This is the closest I have been to a traditional UFO sighting.

Lights in the sky, disk shaped objects, cigar shaped objects, and visitations from alien beings, this is the stuff of which UFO experiences are made. Associated with these are other effects, the electrics in a car are affected so that the lights dim or even go out, the car stops moving, people experience strange shifts in time, people have strange marks on their bodies. All of this is classic psychic stuff: classic daemonic reality, where the experience is both of the mind, of the psyche, and of the physical, of this world. The effect of the car stopping or the mark on the body is physical, and yet after it is over it often disappears as mist on the wind, and only the memory is there to tell you that it happened – or at best a photo, radar or video footage. There are no museums you can go to and see alien craft, or clothing of aliens. All physical evidence disappears behind a smoke screen, often said to be government conspiracy, but a veil of mist nonetheless. The similarities between this and phenomena from the séance room are so striking as to hit one between the eyebrows! There are no museums with ectoplasm, permanent paranormal objects like impossibly linked rings or levitating accordions, but there are hotly disputed photographs, video and tape recordings.

Now I know from my time in stone circles and barrow mounds that time shifts occur in these places, and that these are places where the veils between this world and other realities is very thin. So it is interesting to see that recent research into the GMF aspect of place, and its psi-conducive effects, also links with UFO research.

The Earthlights Hypothesis – UFOs and Geomagnetism

Research into UFOs suggests that some aspects of these, like some polter-geists and our psychic awareness, also appear to be connected with GMF anomaly. In general, overall patterns of UFO sightings are related to earthquake epicentres. The sort of UFO we are talking about here are the lights in the sky variety, not abduction scenarios or any of the more florid forms of UFO. Persinger and Lafrenière[7] analysed a range of UFO and anomalous happenings from the 1960s and 1970s. Their data suggest that UFO phenomena tend to cluster in specific areas. These are called window areas, areas prone to people seeing UFOs. They also often occur in what are called flaps, where you get lots of people reporting a similar experience over a short period of time. UFOs tend to be reported most often in April, July, August and September; which of course could be that people are out more often in the summer months!

Persinger[8] has mapped UFO flaps, such as the Marfa lights in Texas, or lights seen on the West Coast of the United States down the Rocky Mountains. Devereux[9] has done the same with lights seen in Wales, again described by the people seeing them as UFOs, or the famous UFO flap at Warminster in the 1970s. When they stop seeing the lights there is commonly an earth tremor on the fault line on which the place lies just as was found with the BVM in Cairo. Comprehensive maps in Devereux's book show the relationship between UFOs and earthquake epicentres, between UFOs and geological faulting, between UFOs and areas with less thunderstorms than the average, between stone circles, ley lines, UFOs and geological faulting.

Sacred sites, too, are highly correlated with UFO sightings, which occur in window areas, like Croft Hill in Leicestershire, which is composed of granite and syenite and lots of quartz. Devereux found that 50% of the UFO sightings in that area occurred within 10 miles of Croft Hill; 25% within 5 miles. All the UFO sightings were in areas of exceptional geophysical activity, and were at places also associated with abnormal meteorological events like thunderstorms, auroras through to Fortean[10] type events, which encompass such strange events as falls of frogs or fish out of the sky.

(a) Population corrected UFO sightings for England and Wales. The 1971 census map provided the detailed information which allowed the corrections due to population bias to be made. The above map is the result, revealing striking "window" areas.

(b) Earthquake epicentres in England and Wales for the same year. If you imagine laying one map over the other, you see how closely the two mirror each other. (Illustrations courtesy of Paul Devereux. Reproduced from Earthlights by Paul Devereux, Turnstone Press, 1982.)

The core theory[11] for explaining the earthlights aspect of UFOs involves seismo-electricity, that is the electricity that is released by the earth around a geological fault. Not all areas of geological faulting that produce seismic stress will actually move so that we can physically feel it; normally the move is much more subtle than that. During seismic strain, pressure on the rock crystals produces electromagnetic fields through a modification of the piezoelectric effect. The fields created by this process then have electrostatic effects such as ball lightning, will-o'-the-wisps, and other earthquake-related light effects. In other words, earthquakes produce luminous electrical activity; before, during and after the quake electrical discharges to the air take place. However, it is important to remember that mere stress in the rock is sufficient to cause a piezoelectric effect – there doesn't have to be a tremor. Stresses on faults may accumulate over long periods of time. It is while the stress is present that such an effect would be created and phenomena likely to occur. This is the same energy I have talked about earlier that is connected with psychological and psychic effects such as poltergeist outbreaks, haunting, visions of the BVM, and of course faeries; in short this is the energy of the daemonic reality.

Persinger's[12] research has found that when the brain is magnetically stimulated, dreamlike states can occur even in waking consciousness. People experience hallucinations like UFO abduction experiences. Like me he connects this with the limbic system and the pineal gland. Such stimulating fields are not large and could conceivably be produced by transient effects associated with tectonic stress. This links in with all I have said with regard to the pineal gland and psychic events in the first chapter.

While the major source of energy for such a mechanism comes from electrical and magnetic fields associated with geological stress, much smaller displays might be triggered by fields generated by events such as thunderstorms or solar eclipses, or the Northern Lights. Most of us feel the atmosphere just before a thunderstorm – the charge that one gets from the lightning – which may be frightening to some and to others is exhilarating. We are literally charged up by such events.

Lightning always follows the route of lowest electrical resistance, and so can follow some very strange paths! It often strikes preferred trees and places. For instance, there is ten times more lightning over land; and the electrical resistance of oaks is very low and so this is why they are often struck by lightning. Could this be at least partially one of the reasons why pagan people such as Druids hold oaks in such honour? Pointed objects also attract lightning, and there is a suggestion that church steeples were specifically constructed so as to enhance the electrostatic properties of that place. There is a connection here with the pointed hats of witches and wizards, and with the wearing of horns by many an ancient god or goddess, since they are both piezoelectric and pointed.

Lightning is also frequently connected with Fortean type events, such as inexplicable accounts of so-called ball lightning and what is known as St. Elmo's fire, which is a glowing discharge around, for example, ships masts when surrounded by a concentrated and intense electric field. These strange electrical anomalies have been connected both with UFOs and with faery lore.

These earthlights are visible products of an energy that has profound effects on us, taking us into a state of consciousness where we shift between the worlds, see visions and link with the elemental aspect of nature. The sort of visions we see depends on our cultural unconscious; in previous times we connected with earth beings called faeries, these days we connect with space beings called UFOnauts.

UFOs, ley lines, sacred sites, haunting, poltergeists, faery lore and psychic phenomena can all be linked using our knowledge of electro-magnetic, electrostatic and geomagnetic energy. I see this approach as being one facet of the whole; one aspect of our understanding that complements and grounds the mystical, magical, esoteric level of under-standing. And with its links to the hallucinogenic chemicals produced by the pineal gland we can more clearly understand the psychic aspect of UFO experiences and their links with our mythic, dream type state of consciousness. The power of the mind is awesome; what is without is also within, and vice versa; there is an aspect of mind that can manifest physical phenomena and perhaps this is the alien dimension we are contacting when we see UFOs, the modern form of aerial faery.

UFOs and the Psyche

That UFOs are a modern form of faery folk becomes more and more apparent the more I look into it. This is not to say that some UFOs are not nuts and bolts space vehicles and some of their occupants visitors from another star system – some may be, but there is absolutely no way at present of telling – just that some UFOs seem to be connected to energy fields related to the earth, and we perceive them in terms of our cultural mythology. Jung, Vallée, Devereux and others have all considered that the reported form of UFOs and their occupants are created more by our conceptions, by archetypal symbolism, by our 20th century collective unconscious, than by any inherent form in the energy field that we call UFO.

One of the lores of psychology is that we can only perceive that which we can conceive. Something that is totally alien just cannot be seen by us because we have no conception of it. Something that is totally outside our world, or world-view, has nothing with which it can be compared, and if it is at least partly ethereal, then it will be seen according to that image to which it is closest within the person doing the perceiving. Nowadays the collective myth is that of space beings – so we see UFOs – the beings are human like, but alien to us. Nearly all aliens which people have reported seeing have a head with two eyes and a mouth, two arms and two legs. We are remarkably unimaginative!!

The hypothesis is that there is some sort of two-way interaction through psychokinesis between our minds and the energy field of the UFO. In a parapsychological theory called 'Conformance Theory,'[13] it is proposed that the more subtle and sensitive the material, the easier it is for our minds to affect it. It is possible that the energy field we call UFO is a profoundly sensitive energy form, which not only affects us but also is also responsive to our subconscious mental cues. Devereux mentions that with the UFO Foo Fighters in World War 2, which were the first well-known UFOs, 'Some airmen reported that the lights seemed to be responding to their thoughts.'[14]

We are able to create thought forms through vivid visualisation, concentration and emotional energy. This is exactly what is being suggested here. And this is equivalent to the theories underlying certain haunting or apparitions of the BVM – that a place has an energy that we then put a visual and/or auditory image to.

Thus I am suggesting that the geomagnetic anomaly associated with the areas in which UFOs are most commonly found, affects our pineal gland which produces pinoline which takes us into a psi-conducive dream state of consciousness where we are both psychic and 'think' at the collective unconscious level of our mind, in dream images, hallucinations, and archetypal, mythic, primary process thought. It is at this level of our minds that we are most in touch with, or at one with, the world mind, which is manifesting today in UFO form. Thus the UFO energy will respond according to the prevailing conditions, such as how close one is, time of day, ambient electromagnetic conditions, psychic ability of the percipient, and so on.

Many witnesses of UFOs appear to have had a prior psi experience, which suggests that a person who is psychic is more likely to see a UFO. However, with global phenomena like UFOs one is not dealing with a personal, subjective thought form, but an image that is shared by a whole culture – in this case a Westernised global culture since UFOs have been reported mostly in Europe, Russia, North and South America and Australia. UFOs are archetypal for our time. The prevailing imagery of the Westernised global culture of the 20th century means a technological, and more specifically a galactic, outlook – our aliens no

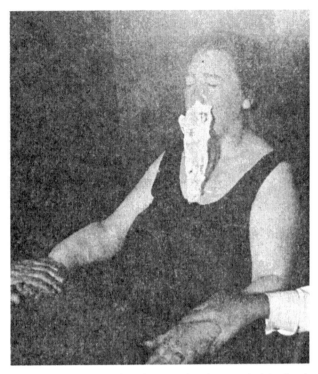

A medium with ectoplasm emerging from her mouth, photographed in October 1929. This is thought to be a semi-physical substance which takes various forms depending on the medium. UFOs seem to be similarly semi-physical with a now-you-see-them-now-you-don't property. (Reproduced from Intention and Survival *by* Glen Hamilton, Regency Press, 1942/1977.)

longer come from Mars – they come from Sirius or Betelgeuse, or whichever other star system is stirring us, like the Pleiades!

Our science fiction is a similar product of our species unconscious imagery. It is remarkable that a science fiction story by Harold Sherman, *The Green Man*,[15] was published in 1946, and this is the prototype of Adamski's UFO encounter. Only a few months separates the publication of this story and the first flying saucer reports by Kenneth Arnold, which started the 20th century phenomenon. And *Twilight Bar*,[16] written by Koestler in 1945, has a UFO causing a blackout, a phenomenon which up until that time had not happened, but which has become quite common since. Our imaginations seem to pave the way for the development of the phenomena and at the same time they also influence human events and destinies, particularly that of those who directly experience the phenomena, or the followers that they may attract as a result of their experiences.

Another interesting point is the types of reports that one gets from the various countries. Thus abduction scenarios were most common in the USA where people are very paranoid about aliens, whether legal or not. In South America people have fantastic experiences; in France they are very civilised; in Britain they are almost matter of fact. These are huge generalisations which one can argue with quite easily in detail, but the general impression that emerges is that national characteristics are present in the sort of experiences people have. Vallée makes this same point: 'In the USA, UFOs appear as SF monsters, in South America they are sanguinary and quick to get into a fight; in France they behave like rational, Cartesian, peace-loving tourists.'[17] Hilary Evans[18] also makes this point very clearly. Earthlights are seen everywhere, but defining them as UFO is a modern Western characteristic. Tribal people will see the phenomena as faeries, or witches, or spirits of the ancestors, or divinities. We humans have a remarkable ability to 'forget all previous appearances and see each new one as separate in and of itself, whereas each form is part of a continuous whole.'[19]

And UFOs also exhibit universal characteristics. The feeling that I have about such things as UFOs and other anomalous phenomena that appear to behave intelligently is that we are dealing with an aspect of the universe itself as an intelligent being, another aspect of Lovelock's Gaia hypothesis,[20] but at a more universal level. We are part of this universe. Our minds are part of the evolving life of this planet, as are the levels of consciousness of other animals, and so just as we embody one form of consciousness evolved on this planet, so the hypothesis that this planet has a sort of world mind that manifests in anomalous ways is a hypothesis that has a certain appeal to it. This planet is part of the solar system, dancing in circles within our galaxy. The holographic universe hypothesis suggests that at the psychic level we are all interlinked, so our planetary consciousness is at one level one with the world mind. This is what is meant by the spirit world, the other world, the daemonic reality.

Devereux suggests that the UFO phenomenon is a sort of planetary ectoplasm, a quasi-physical substance which can take on whatever form our consciousness puts into it. And remember we can understand the alien in terms of inner as well as outer space – there are more things in our mind than we are aware of – and our mind can act as a totally independent being. As Devereux so cynically says:

'On the one hand the mysteries of the universe can be reflected back to the stunned conscious mind of the witness, while on the other – a far more common occurrence – all that is displayed are elements from the common cultural ethos, usually in the comic-strip media imagery that has now become the mental currency for keeping our collective beliefs, fears and dreams alive. If the UFO pageant today resembles nothing more than the incoherent ravings of a fevered mind, than that is the true reflection of our current collective mental situation.'[21]

Points of Correspondence Between UFOs and Faery Reality

One of the suggestions proposed by Vallée[22] is that there exists a natural phenomenon whose manifestations border on both the physical and the mental. There is a medium in which human dreams can be implemented, and this is the mechanism by which UFO events are generated. The experience frequently incorporates sexual and genetic aspects, which reinforce it by connecting it with our most powerful emotions, those linked to species survival.

I have already mentioned the similarities in form between UFO beings and the fair folk. Vallée points out even more correspondences between the modern UFO scenario and the traditional faery. In both experiences one gets experiences regarding food, such as getting people to cook for them, or taking food from people, or giving food to people, such as magical oatmeal jars that are always full. A Roman writer, Porphyry, mentions an interesting little snippet of information: 'All the various gods, genii or daemons, enjoy as nourishment the odour of burnt offerings.'[23] Burn the toast and give it to the faeries; which sheds a completely different light on the story of Alfred the Great and the burnt griddle cakes. Also, the fragments which fell to the floor after a meal were believed in the Highlands to belong to the faeries

There is the same sort of behaviour, the same fugitiveness and the same ignorance of logical or physical laws as you get in dreams. Both fair folk and UFO beings seem to be renowned as thieves taking plants, animals (dogs, cattle, horses) and people. Animals are often terrified, running from craft, as they have good cause to be because one also gets reports of animal mutilations in both sets of lore.

Another strange aspect is that they always speak the native language. They do not speak to scientists and they do not send sophisticated signals in codes. They speak to ordinary local people. They say they are superior. They can comfort and they can terrify, they sometimes stand for justice and right and say they are good. They appear in different forms and speak with telepathy – you hear the words inside your head separate from them. They often lie or give misleading information. This keeps scientists away and gives the UFO myth its religious and mystical overtones.

There is an historical development in UFO stories, from biblical accounts onwards, and in all cultures, e.g. Ezekiel from the traditional Hebrew culture, Quetzalcoatl from the traditional Mexican. In more modern times, Vallée points out that this is illustrated by the UFOs progressing from the aerial ships of the 1890s, to dirigibles, to ghost rockets to flying saucers. However, the mechanism of the experience in all these times is standard and follows the model of all psychic phenomena. As Vallée[24] notes, apparitions of the BVM are basically UFO phenomena where the entity has delivered a message to do with religious beliefs rather than with fertilisers or engineering, or the various other mundane messages that are so often reported, though many modern UFO messages are of a religious nature.

We are now a culture that does not in general believe in faeries, though recently there has started to be a resurgence in faery and angelic belief. However, many do believe in UFOs, not as a nebulous mythic something, but as a nuts and bolts spacecraft coming from another star system or galaxy with technologically superior people, which means they must be more powerful than us. Some then feel they must be wiser than us, others feel they must be more rapacious than us. How they experience the alien is dependent on how they have experienced superior beings, their parents and teachers, when they were children, or how they perceive their culture to be and the people in power. Are our governments primarily wise or are they self seeking, rapacious, inconsiderate of the needs of the people? The mythology of the UFOs says an awful lot about how people perceive the culture in which they are living.

So here is an alternative scenario for the modern UFO abduction experience. Rather than seeing it as a physical occurrence inside a space-craft, we can understand it as the person experiencing a temporary altera-tion of their consciousness into the psychic, or daemonic, reality in which they experience visions of archetypal creatures, rather like a poltergeist experience. This takes into account the often absurd, dreamlike elements of people's UFO experiences.

As Vallée says: 'There is a system around us that transcends time and space. What we see here is not an alien invasion. It is a spiritual system that acts on and uses humans. The UFO phenomenon represents evidence for other dimensions beyond space–time – a multiverse. The UFOs are physical manifestations that simply cannot be understood apart from their psychic and symbolic reality. UFOs are real physical objects yet they are not ET spacecrafts – the ET theory is not strange enough to explain the facts.'[25] Consciousness and paranormal phenomena like UFOs are one of its manifestations.

As an example, one of the classic stories of UFO abductions concerns Barney and Betty Hill. They were abducted into a spacecraft and one of

(a) Fairies revelling inside a tumulus; notice the similarity in shape with a modern UFO, and the light spilling out from the tumulus. (Illustration by George Cruikshank. Reproduced from The Fairy Mythology *by Thomas Keightley, London, 1850.)*

(b) A representation of a UFO, drawn to illustrate the encounter by Betty and Barney Hill in 1961. Notice the shape, the light and the pixie like occupants. (Illustration reproduced from UFO: The Complete Sightings Catalogue *by Peter Brookesmith, Blandford Press, 1995.)*

the things that happened was that Betty was shown a star map – but it was a star map to nowhere and to everywhere; it was not a real map with coordinates so you could definitely find a particular point in the sky and say this is where it relates to. The map must have been placed there for Betty Hill to see, not for the pilot to use. People will be able to argue forever as to the whereabouts of that star map. It will be applicable to any and everybody's belief system; we can all read what we like into it.

This is exactly the same as, for example, Nostradamus'[26] prophecies which are eternal and for all people, because anyone can read into them whatever suits their belief system – before they have been decoded anyway. Hindsight gives perfect vision. The same applies with much fortune telling, channelling and mediumistic communication; frequently it is so nebulous that you can interpret it according to your circumstances, your attitudes, and your needs. It is not fixed into any one definite thing. In parapsychology this even has a name, 'The Barnum Effect,'[27] after the Victorian American showman Barnum who said: 'There's a sucker born every minute.' Research has shown that there are certain statements that apply to everyone. For instance, imagine that you are at a fairground and I am reading your palm. I look at it for a few minutes, then I look up at you with great sympathy and say: 'Life has been really difficult recently, but it will be getting better.' Most people will respond to that statement with 'Yes, life has been difficult recently,' because for most of us life tends to be difficult most of the time. And we're only too happy to hear that it's going to be getting better.

This is not to say that all psychic utterances are only Barnum statements: there are many strikingly accurate telepathic, clairvoyant and precognitive accounts in the annals of psychic research, and we just need to be wary of them, and not read great wisdom into everything that appears to come from a discarnate source. The daemonic reality is well known for its trickster qualities. It'll make fun whenever it can. I must repeat, I am not saying UFO experiences are not real. I am saying they are a psychophysical, mind–matter interface called the daemonic reality.

Abductions and Changelings

Witchfinders searched witches for a scar or mark as proof of them having contact with the devil; abductees prove their experiences by showing scars or marks. Hypnosis can produce scars and marks in the body. Stigmatics, through their deep devotion to the passion of Christ, produce wounds in their hands and feet that can bleed copiously. Many children who remember a previous lifetime have birthmarks connected with their mode of death in that previous life. Physical effects on the body are linked with emotional, psychological and psychic experiences. The mind is perfectly capable of affecting the body in any way it wants.

Our medical technology is far in advance of the experiences reported by abductees, which is more like folk knowledge of medicine. An example of such an experience was told to me by a Finnish lady at a conference. She was awakened one night and found herself taken into a UFO ship where she was examined on a hospital-type couch. She was then implanted with a foetus. Several months later she once again awoke at night to have a similar experience but in this case the foetus was removed. No doctor need induce such trauma in hundreds of patients just to collect a little blood, a few embryos. It is very clear here that the interaction is a symbolic one. On a psychic/spiritual level the implantation of the foetus is the implantation of the spiritual within humanity for the evolution of our consciousness. It seems that modern UFO abduction experiences, where the person is impregnated, are symbolic of a reawakening of spirituality within the most material of all human cultures, the Western civilisation. In times of faery belief, people actually gave birth to the faery children, and I have noticed among many of the young mothers today a similar sort of belief arising again, in that the child is felt to be an old soul, or to have faery characteristics in one way or another.

The abduction experience is a very similar experience to that concerning faeries where kidnapping also occurred. Most frequently they abducted a nursing mother to suckle one of their own, or a midwife to help at the birthing. This is a tradition found around the world, indicating an ancient belief that if supernaturals were to partake of mortal milk they would acquire some sort of vigour or life they needed in order to exist here, or to connect with the physical plane – as though they needed that extra physical dimension, being in themselves too ethereal for this plane of existence. Men who were kidnapped tended to be pipers, minstrels, etc. who returned with the gift of faery music in their hands.

Women who nurse faery children are often given a salve to rub on the child's eyes; if by chance they rub it on their own, they find that they can then see the faeries at any time. Nearly always when the faeries find out that this has happened they spit on her eye and so blind her. Invisibility is a typical faery art – the faery mist. Certain elves appear to be permanently invisible unless one has a talisman or spell by which they can be seen. Others have a hat or cloak that make them invisible, e.g. mantle of Manannan. Tolkien uses this in *Lord of the Rings*,[28] with the ring making its wearer invisible, which is classic. In the Scottish highlands, 'fith-fath' is an incantation or word–spell which can render the speaker invisible or transform a person or object into another form, e.g. human into animal.

If you sleep on a faery mound you are likely to be captured and taken below. A kidnapped person could revisit human places after seven years, as in the beautiful song about Tam Lin, from Northumberland. In this case Tam is rescued by a woman who falls in love with him having seen him as she slept under a faery tree one afternoon, but generally the abductee finds it impossible to readjust and returns to the faery world. Often only the spirit of the person is taken, leaving the body in a coma.

A changeling was a faery child who had been exchanged in the night for one's own human child, sometimes by a monstrous red hand which came through the roof whilst they were sleeping, but also stolen by the fays when their mothers were out working in the fields. In some cases the fay left a piece of wood, which was given volition, and the semblance of humanity by faery magic in place of the human child. They sometimes also did this when capturing women, such as the midwife.

The changeling was known by its wan and wrinkled appearance, its long fingers and bony body, its fractious behaviour and voracious appetite, its large teeth and fondness for music and dancing. A changeling might be tricked into betraying itself by doing an unusual act, e.g. boiling water in eggshells, which the changeling then reacted to by saying that he had seen a certain forest grow and die three times but had never seen such a thing before. This takes us back to the time shift aspect of faery which I talked about in the previous chapter. An elvish cast of eye is witness to the faery paternity of an infant, also pointed ears like those of Puck – or Spock. This is linked with ideas relating to the evil eye, or its opposite the beneficent eye, the power of the gaze as every lover knows – or the jealous glance. There's more to eyes than we have yet discovered. The retina is literally part of the brain extruded out. And there is also a special nerve that goes from the retina to the pineal gland, the seat of the soul. I feel that looking in to someone's eyes is like looking into their soul. And recently there have been experiments on the power of staring, of which more later. I have a fascinating Victorian book called *The Evil Eye*,[29] which talks about many superstitions and beliefs closely related to the faery lore, which includes goddess lore, horned beings, through to charms and hand gestures.

There are several theories regarding the lore about changelings: one is that some of the faery tales are remnants of tales about the Neolithic people. These people were conquered by the invading Bronze Age Celts and retreated to the hills and wilder places. Intermarriage between the two races inevitably occurred. The Celts considered the

The Tuatha de Danaan riding in procession, typical of the fair folk of human stature, the shining ones. (Illustration courtesy of Alan Lee. Reproduced from Fairies *by Brian Froud and Alan Lee, Pan Books, 1979.)*

original inhabitants with some awe. Because of the magnificent megalithic monuments which they had created, they were considered to be magic beings, so marriage with them gave magic powers to the children.

Another theory is that of reincarnation: the ancestors steal the souls of people, and substitute one of themselves. Spence[30] thinks that originally the belief was not associated with abduction, but rather with the notion that ancestral spirits awaiting rebirth ensouled the bodies of

newborn infants of their own kindred. A large number of changelings when discovered appear as old men who appear to know the area from times long past. Such a changeling is obviously the ancestral spirit of a distant generation, an old soul. This, in time, after the encroaches by Christianity and through a confusion of mental processes, was exchanged for a belief that the spirits of the ancestors actually took an infant's body.

The ancient belief is that soul and body are as one. When an individual falls sick, their soul has been carried off by some bad spirit —

a spirit interpretation of what today is called out-of-body or near-death experience. To overcome the bad spirit is the first task of healing that the shaman, or witch, must perform before healing at any other level can occur.

Marriage

Linked with the theme of abduction and changelings is that of marriage. There are many tales that concern marriage between a faery and a mortal. The Forest of Dean had tall and dignified beings who married with local chieftains. Children of such marriages are renowned for the second sight, which could be the origin of the supposed hereditary witch families, those families that seem to have psychic abilities as a hereditary trait. How many of us have faery blood?

Such a union was hedged round by rigid taboos. The mortal lover must not reveal his association with his fay mistress, or allude to her fay nature, or touch her with iron. The fay mistress must be permitted to retire from the public gaze at certain times. If any of these happened she would disappear, sometimes with any children she had borne. She often gave him a gift which protected him. A classic example is the tale of the McLeods of Dunvegan who were helped by a fay woman. Dunvegan is a castle on the Isle of Skye in the Inner Hebrides of Scotland. It is said that one of the McLeod chiefs married a faery woman and she had a child. After the birth she left, her husband escorting her to the faery bridge with great sadness, but accepting her wish to depart. That evening during the feast celebrating the birth of the baby, the nurse left the baby so she could listen to the music. The McLeod chief saw her and asked her to bring the baby and she rushed back hoping all was well. Whilst she had been away the baby had woken and cried and 'dear as her earth-born child was to her heart, by eldritch means (the mother) hastened to be beside him and comfort him when no one else was near. She might not take him in her arms; but instead she spread over him a shining faery covering of grass-green silk, embroidered with elf spots and wrought with unearthly skill.'[31] The nurse took the babe and cover down to the hall and all the people heard faery music and the words of the three boons to the McLeods saying that if ever the McLeods were in need that they could raise this as a banner and the faery hosts would come to their aid. Twice the McLeods were saved, once in battle and once when the cattle had the murrain (foot and mouth). But in 1799 a factor called Buchanan broke open the box and took the banner out to see if the curse was real, and the curse fell on the McLeods, so that the heir died, they who lost most of their lands, and the family died out to the point where there were not enough men left to row a boat over the loch. The banner is still to be seen in a glass case at Dunvegan castle.

Most parts of Britain had such marriage practices, and in fact most tales have the elfin lover in this world, rather than the human going to faeryland, such as in *The King of Elfland's Daughter*.[32] In this beautiful tale, the local prince marries the faery princess and she lives with him and has children by him, but her father misses her and eventually by magic succeeds in luring her back to faeryland.

In Ireland, the fair folk of human stature, who are linked with the Celtic gods and goddesses, are called the Tuatha de Danaan as they are the people of the great Irish goddess Dana. They ruled Ireland before the Celts who defeated them in battle. The Tuatha women married the Irish Kings and so continued to rule Ireland for many generations after the Sons of Mil had conquered Ireland. Many of the Irish tales are about the Celtic heroes who had to prove their worth in order to marry the Tuatha woman who embodied the spirit of the land. By being courteous, kind, caring, etc., so he proves himself a man worthy to take on the stewardship of the land. And so their descendants ruled after they had left this world for faeryland. The line was matriarchal and although the Bronze Age Celts had nominally won the Isle, the Tuatha continued to govern through the women. This is the essence of goddess worshipping matriarchy which seems to be the hallmark of the Neolithic people. The Picts in Scotland were also matriarchal. Obviously the fay are both male and female, but female fair folk stand out in the folklore partly to glorify the male Celtic hero by his association with them, and partly because many of the ancient goddesses survived as fair folk.

The faery records of Wales abound in legends of elfin sweethearts, e.g. Pwyll and Rhiannon, The Green Knight, the tale of Melusine. In Scotland, the most famous is that of Thomas the Rhymer, who lived for seven years with the faery queen. In general the faery women made the first advance to her prospective lover, which again suggests a remnant of the old pre-Celtic matriarchal culture.

Sometimes the faery lady appeared to her lover in the guise of a deer, hare or other animals, as in the story of Finn Mac Cumhal (pronounced Cooal) and his faery wife Sava, who was first seen by him as a deer. This is a classic shapeshifting magical attribute which shows the deep connection with nature. This is an animistic religion, one in which all things have their spiritual aspect and we link with the spirit, the attributes, of that particular animal. Nowadays, the divination cards featuring animals, devised by Jamie Sams and David Carson,[33] are very popular, because they have this totemic, archetypal aspect which is missing in the traditional Western systems such as the Tarot. Our culture has denigrated nature, denigrated that mythical aspect of our being. The faery renews it, as in the beautiful silke stories of Scotland in which the faery woman takes the form of a seal, and the man who would wed her must take and keep her seal skin if she is to stay with him. When, inevitably, she finds her skin then she returns to the sea.

Occasionally mortal women had faery men as lovers, but this seems to be far less common. Often this form of connection is surrounded by problems such as the wife wanting to know his name, the lover disappearing and the woman spending years and many trials searching for him. A Greek example of this classic myth is that of Eros and Psyche, and the archetypal aspect is that as humans if we would aspire to divinity, then we have many lessons, trials and tribulations which are all food for the growth of the soul. Often girls were abducted to be wed to the faery king, which has such a resonance to modern UFOlogy as to be quite spooky!

The Archetypal in the UFO

UFOs provide the physical support for our own archetypal dreams. We do the rest. UFO beings tend to be humanoid, able to breathe our air, walk normally on our planet, speak our language (whatever language we may speak!). The same applies to elves and angels, sylphs and djinn. Therefore they cannot be literally visitors from other planets because there are too many landings – an estimated 3 million in the past two decades. This number is totally absurd. Further, the behaviour of UFOs is contrary to what physical objects do: it is the behaviour of an image or a holographic projection, yet the objects leave material traces as did the materialised limbs of mediumistic séances: psychic mind-over-matter effects.

The attitude of the authorities is an important component of the UFO phenomenon. Could it be that the reaction of our society to suppress the reports, to cover them up is as much a part of the phenomenon as the objects themselves, the same as is done with reports of seeing faeries, or reports of physical phenomena at séances, or reports of hauntings or poltergeist phenomena. Our society is scared of these outbreaks of the daemonic into our rational world and so defends against it by scorn, denial and repression. An example that readily comes to mind is the prosecution of the medium Helen Duncan in the 1950s, the last person to be tried under the witchcraft laws, which after that trial were repealed and changed to the Fraudulent Mediums Act. Helen Duncan was found guilty of faking the ectoplasmic phenomena at her séances, but the case is still disputed. And people who witness such phenomena often rationalise the experience away, even to the point of later denying that they witnessed what at the time they said had occurred.

As Vallée says: 'The UFO evokes a deep emotional reaction in the viewer but logical development of an investigation is prevented or precluded by the apparent violations of causality that surround it and by the sociological climate that is created. The lurid aspects of many such stories – and the ridiculous, e.g. pancakes given by aliens! make their serious examination improbable and this reinforces the role of the rumours as folklore, rich in new images.'[34]

The central myth is contact between humans and aliens – a spectrum of experience from abduction to exposure of humanoids, to reports of aliens. A subculture now exists in every country with respect to the aliens. UFO contact changes people's lives. Are we slipping towards a new form of religion, a new spiritual movement? With every new wave of sightings the social impact becomes greater. More people become fascinated with space, with new frontiers in consciousness.

'Whether the creatures come down in flying saucers or in musical baskets, whether they come out of the sea or the rock, is irrelevant. What IS relevant is what they say and do: the trace that they leave in the human witness who is the only tangible vehicle of the story.'[35] This is true of all mediumistic trance messages, poltergeist and haunting experiences, and the modern channellings. In themselves they are frequently puerile and senseless, sometimes they contain wisdom, but they all leave an impact on those who experience the phenomena, out of all proportion to the message. The impact is that of communication with non-human reality – that there is something other than this physical world, that there is an otherworld, another dimension, spirits, divinity, whatever, and we are in contact with it. It is interesting that channelling is contact with spirit – not spirits of the dead as in mediumistic communication but supposedly wise, ethereal beings who may never have lived. We must take responsibility for our visions and our voices. Just because we channel something verbally or visually does not mean that it is good or right. We can channel or experience garbage far more easily than we can channel wisdom, because it all so easily gets coloured by our own personality and our cultural beliefs and prejudices.

Each UFO, or faery, or poltergeist, or mediumistic, or channelling event is unique and yet corresponds to a general pattern; each event is unique and yet there are patterns that distinguish poltergeist from haunting, and so on. The primary point is that the phenomena vary according to our totally unconscious culture and environment. Whether we experience faery, or UFO or poltergeist depends on the circumstances in which we find ourselves and our deeply held beliefs.

Types of sightings of the fair folk arise from a sort of mental suggestion from that earth energy or intelligence we call faery acting on the percipients subliminal mind. This mental mystical part of the planet is always there, merely changing its form every so often. UFOs are faeries in modern guise, representing in outer form the subconscious archetype of our planetary mind at this time – contact with other beings in the Universe.

The thesis that I am suggesting here is that some UFOs are aerial energies that we react to psychically, hallucinating imagery that reflects our times, which links us with our collective unconscious, and so the imagery seen is archetypally important for us. Once again we are in contact with the daemonic, the psychophysical reality that is both of, and not of, this earthly realm.

4

Divinity: Our Link
with the Otherworld

*Faeryland exists as a supernormal state of consciousness into which
men and women may enter temporarily in dreams, trances or
various ecstatic condition; or for an indefinite period at death.*

   *Though it seems to surround it and interpenetrate this planet
even as the X-rays interpenetrate matter, it can have no other
limits than those of the universe itself.*

(Lady Gregory, 1979)[1]

Mythology

So far we have been looking at the magic of faery, the psychic-physical
aspect of the daemonic reality, which is central to this particular philosophy, and starting to see how this is an archetypal reality, the stuff of
myth. It is through these daemonic beings that we interact with the
divine. This is such an important point to the whole of my thesis. At
one level we can understand ley lines, sacred sites, UFOs, hauntings,
ghosts as some sort of electromagnetic earth energy that affects us physically, emotionally, mentally and psychically. At another level we can
understand it as the spirit of the place which we interact with at a
mythic archetypal dream level. And in understanding UFOs in this
light we are seeing that in any belief we create a mythology. UFOs
conform to a basic faery mythology, the mythology of the alien otherworld, which is psychic in its very nature. Those people who believe
that UFOs are nuts and bolts spacecraft are very much part of our
Western world in which only the material is real, and so for UFOs to
be real they have to be material. In the faery faith, the psychic realm is
as real as the material, and so the reality of UFOs is not dependent on
them being material, whilst acknowledging the material aspect of that
experience as well as, the type of experiences people are having is mythological. The UFO beings come from elsewhere, they are powerful, they

85

adopt a certain form, they intermingle with humans, they impart good or evil. All this mythology is straight out of faery.

There is a suggestion that one thread in the tales of the fair folk is that of the Neolithic people who built the stone circles. I think that when we look at the faery faith we are looking at the philosophy, the spirituality of these people. In the course of time, some of these beings assumed semi-divine status, as with the Tuatha de Danaan (Children of the goddess Dana) in Ireland, and the Twlwth Teg (Shining Ones) in Wales, and in British mythology, the divinity of Albion.

This is the next aspect of the faery faith that I wish to look at. Like most children in Britain, I was brought up with Greek (Aesop's fables), Danish (Hans Christian Andersen), and German (Brothers Grimm) mythology. Every myth has its teaching, its morality and ethics, an understanding of human nature and the growth of the soul. What has been buried and forgotten is the Celtic, and I believe that each mythology is appropriate for the land that it springs from. For some reason the mythology of Britain has been forgotten by the people who live in that land, and I think that this means that in some way the soul of Britain, the spirit of Britain has gone underground. I want to bring it back into our awareness, so that we can once again grow and develop and learn in tune with this spirit.

I can talk about the Celtic, because that is what I have been studying for the past twenty years, but my understanding is that the mythology of the Celtic tales matches closely the mythological aspects of faery that are found the world over. For example, the Australian Aboriginal spirit race are similar to British faeries in that they are always youthful, frequent sacred sites, are only seen by psychics, control human affairs and natural phenomena, and are real invisible entities who must be propitiated if people wish to secure their goodwill. They are beneficent, protective beings when not offended and may attach themselves to individuals as guardian spirits. Spirit beings are found all over Africa, Asia, China, Japan and India. There are Greek nereids and nymphs, Arabian djinns and afreets.

In this way, the mythic archetypes of the Celtic people link with the collective unconscious and animistic spirituality all over the planet. This perennial philosophy underlying all the world religions is to be found in the folk tales of spirits, of elementals, the giants of the hilltops, the ladies of the lakes. It is this animistic philosophy which I see re-emerging in the modern faery faith. It is a world view in which spirit is immanent – everything material has its spirit aspect – so a glass in the material is the container for my drink, and the glass in the spiritual is that aspect which is the cup of love, the fount which flows over, heart, emotion and this glass becomes a chalice that is used in sacred ceremony. So a tree is just a tree and it is also a being that is maybe 500 years old with its own particular 'energy', its spirit, which can be very healing if you sit under it and relax and feel the presence of this ancient still being. This is the essence of devic and totemic belief, that all living things have their spirit aspect, and we interact with the world with this in full awareness. Why is a fly bothering me, what is the spirit of this pesky creature? I treat the world very differently when I interact with it in this way. I don't just carve through a hill with huge machines, or cut down trees just to make some money, because I am aware of the energy that the hill gives to the surrounding land – the beauty of it that soothes the heart and lifts the soul, that gives our spirits a lift when we are feeling down.

Where I live, in Glastonbury, there is the spirit of the Tor, called Gwynn ap Nudd. He has his faery castle here, and not only that but the Tor is the entrance to Annwn which is the Welsh otherworld, and under-world, and in order to enter this place one has to cross two rivers, a river of water and a river of blood. Strangely at the foot of the Tor are two springs, a white spring which flows out of the limestone of the Tor and calcifies all it passes, creating amazing beautiful chalky shapes, and the Chalice Well, which is iron rich and runs blood red. If you look at the shape of the Tor, Chalice Hill and the other hills of Avalon from the south, it seems as if it the shape of a woman/goddess lying on her back, with the Tor her breast, Chalice Hill her pregnant belly and Wearyall Hill her thigh and knee. Where the two springs rise is just below the breast on the left side – exactly where you find the heart. There is a myth that Joseph of Arimathea came to Glastonbury bearing two cruets with him, a cruet of blood and a cruet of water, which flowed out of Jesus after he was pierced with the spear. These flowed from that precise place – the heart just under the breast on the left side of the body, just where the two springs flow in the body of the land called Avalon. This is legend, this is myth, a land which embodies the sacred, a land which takes you into the otherworld, a land where the elementals are strong, where psychic experiences are common and where the gods reside. When we consider the faery faith we are not only connecting with a psychic reality, we are connecting the reality of divinity, the divinity that is this particular piece of this beautiful planet.

In theory psychic phenomena are integral to the divine. Take clairvoyance for example – in theory there are as yet no known limits. The furthest humans have gone is to the moon. An astronaut, Edgar Mitchell,[2] did some ESP experiments whilst orbiting the moon. There were interesting results, suggestive of clairvoyance. Obviously more research needs to be done before we can say whether or not clairvoyance can happen over such a large distance, but it has not been ruled out. Perhaps people will go to Mars and perhaps once again it will be found that clairvoyance occurs. Perhaps we will travel to the other side of the universe. Perhaps through telepathy, clairvoyance, precognition and the other psychic arts we can, in potential, be aware of anything in the universe that ever has been, is, or will be. This is called in parapsychology, the super-ESP hypothesis. It is also an attribute of divinity – omniscience. This is the faery faith.

Animism

The essence of animism is the Great Chain of Being. This philosophy says that spirit is immanent in all things and that the highest ideal is spirit and in between there is a chain of being from matter, to life, to mind, to soul to spirit. It goes back to the dawning of consciousness when humans began to personalise the manifestations of Nature. Its twin deities are the two main concepts of male and female deities which are found in the pantheons of nearly all religions; which Carl Jung[3] calls the archetypes of the Collective Unconscious.

Central to modern pagan mythology is the Great Mother. Research shows that in former times worship of Her spanned the world, and Her names are as innumerable as are the aspects under which she was adored – Hecate, Artemis, Isis, Brigid, Diana, Ashara, Ishtar, Cybele, Cerridwen, Hera, Mary, are but a few. And in the course of time the Great Mother was joined by the god her consort, or lover or son, sometimes all three. They are personifications of the pairs of opposites, which manifest in the world of form; of light and dark, summer and winter, life and death, seed time and harvest.

In one of her aspects the Great Mother was revered as the Moon Goddess. The moon was thought to govern fertility; her light was the creative agent. This ancient belief is beginning now to find scientific confirmation with bio-dynamic agriculturists studying the effects of planting seeds at different phases of the moon, of harvesting herbs at different phases. Similarly Dr. Jonas[4] in Czechoslovakia has been having success with birth control and fertility problems by utilising astrological charts and phases of the moon. The moon has also been found to link in some way with psychic phenomena. Radin[5] worked for a few years at the University of Nevada in Las Vegas, and his laboratory was funded by one of the casinos. They let him look at four years' worth of their accounts and he found that over those four years there had been six jackpots on the one armed bandits. Every single jackpot occurred at a full moon. Similarly with the other games, the greatest payouts occurred in the week either side of the full moon, depending on the

Isis with the sun between her moon-like horns. She is the archetypal mother goddess in all her beauty and power. There were Isis temples until about 600AD. (Reproduced from Egyptian Mythology *by Veronica Ions, Hamlyn, 1975.)*

game either just before or just after. He also found that winnings on the lotteries tended to peak in the week leading up to the dark moon.

The consort of the Goddess was the horned god of nature known in northern Europe as Cernunnnos, who is the horned god of Gaul; or Herne the Hunter, or the Cerne Abbas giant in England (think of the Scottish ch-sound to find the link between these three names); as the Minotaur, Dionysius and Pan by the Greeks, who is first encountered

Cernunnos, the protoype of the horned god and forerunner of Herne the Hunter, as depicted on the Gundestrup cauldron from the 1st millenium BCE in the Nationalmuseet, Copenhagen. (Reproduced from The Illustrated Golden Bough *by J.G. Frazer, Macmillan/ Book Club Associates, 1978.)*

in the 5th century BCE. In the Bronze Age the figures may be either male or female, and the horns are those of cattle, sheep or goats. The horns were a sign of divinity, and this god was a most potent god. A most interesting survival into modern times of the Horned God is the Puck Fair of Killorglin, County Kerry, Eire, which takes place at Lammas (August 1st).

He was the god of hunting; the woods and the fields were his. He ruled the horned beasts and thus was the god of farmers and shepherds. In some cases he was the god of death. It is possible that the Christian Church, in attempting to eradicate the former religion, created their devil in the guise of the former god, but one must not see in every horned idol a representation of the devil. Nowadays he is being reborn as the Green Man, an archetype for men to connect with, who is of Nature, rather than of war, and men are mixing the two images together in a very interesting rebirth of this most ancient of archetypes.

Every aspect of matter has its spirit. The size of the fair folk varies from thumb size to human stature depending on type and era. I have just talked about the fair folk of larger stature who are the ancient gods. The diminutive forms are the devic aspects of faery. Devas are the spirits of nature, the ground of all being, the most common being the flower faery. Shape shifting by magic may partially explain the variations in size, but there are also different types of faery, as I hope by now you are beginning to recognize. The belief in the fluid nature of spirit underlies this. For example, sea gods particularly are prone to shape shifting which reflects the ever-changing character of their element, whilst the earth spirits are more stable in their form.

Elementals are the spirit of that particular element. Think of the awesome power of an earthquake, a tidal wave, a volcano, a hurricane and you can begin to feel the spirit of each element. There are four kinds of elemental or devic faery, according to the four elements:

Earth – gnomes, goblins, pixies, corrigans, leprechauns, and some elves.
Air – sylphs, aerials, flower faeries;
Water – undines, lake faeries;
Fire – will-o'-the-wisps, salamanders (seldom found in Celtic Faith.)

Different types represent specific strata of our subliminal cultural imagination. The power of nature from flower faeries, through water sprites, sylphs and undines, spirits of fire and of water, to the great giants of earth such as Gog and Magog of Britain, is immanent and is the basis of animism, and totemism in which the spirit of animal is revered.

This elemental aspect of faery is central to the growing spirituality of this day, an example being the modern day myth of Findhorn, which has inspired so many people during the past three decades. At Findhorn[6] in the 1970s giant cabbages grew. Not for long, but for long enough for a myth of working with devic elemental energies to arise and inspire many to the belief that we can link with these energies, with the spirits of the land, we can work with them. This is classic faery faith mythology, and it is the faery in everyday life.

Part of animistic lore is that it is considered unlucky to speak the genuine names of supernaturals, as this was believed to offend them and tempt their vengeance. Thus traditionally there are many names for faeries such as: good folk, wee folk, seely folk, good neighbours, pechs, pixie, piskie, pook. In the Scottish Highlands and in Ireland, the faeries were known as the sidhe (hill folk – the dwellers within the hills or mounds). It is implicit in animistic belief that the name of a man or spirit is a vital part of the individual – to know it and pronounce it presumes power over the person or spirit to whom it belongs. If a human learns a faery's name the faery is bound to undertake any task which the human wishes, or free them from any vow they have made to the faery, e.g. Rumpelstiltskin. It is the exception outside Ireland to find a definite name and personality assigned to members of the faery world. Some faery ladies even refused to acquaint their mortal husbands with their name, and the same applies to some faery husbands. Those fair folk whose names we do know are those who have godlike attributes, e.g. Arianrhod, Gwynn, Oberon, etc.

Walking Between the Worlds

When we connect with divinity we connect with the otherworld, for divinity lives both in this world and in the otherworld, whether that world is conceived of as a heaven or hell, over the seas or under the earth or up in the skies, it is not of this on-the-earth world that we inhabit. It is separated from us it is other, and in the faery faith mythology it is possible for us to visit this otherworld.

The Irish know it as Tir-na-Nog – the land over the oceans to the West. There is a wonderful faery tale about a princess whose brothers had been turned into swans by a wicked queen and only for ten days in the year, the longest days at the summer solstice, could they visit this world. During the night they regained their human form and the princess met with them. She asked them how she could overcome the spell and they told her that she had to make them nettle shirts and throw these over them. They flew with her over the oceans to the West, to the other-world where they lived. After many trials and tribulations in which she nearly died at the stake she managed to make the shirts, and of course married the prince of that land.

Often the entrance to the otherworld is a hill. Glastonbury Tor is one example, another is the Eildon Hills in Scotland. And sometimes you enter the otherworld by passing through a fog or mist, as Cormac did when lured there by Manannan mac Lir, who is the Irish equivalent to Gwynn.

This is a classic tale about the greatest initiation of all – to travel to the otherworld and back in full consciousness. The shamanic peoples who live an animistic spirituality honour their shamans highly for this is their art, to be able to walk between the worlds in full consciousness. This is our birthright. In this tale Cormac, High King of Ireland, was out walking on the land of Tara, when a grey-bearded man came into view carrying a silver branch that tinkled as he walked and the sweetness of its music was such that all cares and grief were driven away. Cormac spoke with this man and asked for the branch, which the man gave him on condition that Cormac would give to him three things when they were asked for. Cormac agreed, and the following week the man came to him and asked for his son. Cormac gave his son, and all the people of Tara were horror-struck and loudly wailed their lament that the son of Cormac was lost, but Cormac shook the silver branch and the grief was forgotten. A month passed, and once again the man appeared and asked for Cormac's daughter. Cormac gave her to the man and once again the people of Tara cried aloud in their sorrow at the loss of the daughter of Cormac, but he shook the branch and they forgot their sorrow. A year passed and the man appeared and claimed the wife of Cormac, and this time Cormac followed the man who disappeared into a mist. Emerging from the mist, he found himself in Tir-na-Nog, the land of eternal youth and beauty where the salmon swims in the pool of the fount of life feeding on the nuts of the hazel tree. There were women awaiting Cormac, and they bathed him in this pool and took him into the great hall where Manannan, for this was the old grey-haired man, was seated at the table with his family. He welcomed Cormac and praised him and said that he would give him the cup of truth for having passed through the veils in full consciousness. So Cormac returned to Tara with his family and whoever drank of that cup spoke truly and wisely.

The Cup of Truth is a symbol of having gained knowledge of the mystery of life and death, and the Apple Branch is a symbol of the peace and joy which comes to all who are truly initiated. In Scotland all the witches who were burned during the witch hunts said that they had obtained their knowledge through their relationship with the fair folk. Thomas the Rhymer is said to have lived with the faery queen in the Eildon Hills (in the border country between Scotland and England) for seven years. When he returned he had the gift of prophecy, so he was also called True Thomas. This ability to visit the spirit world at will is considered to be the highest initiation, and is the training which the shaman is taught. Some cultures consider one needs to spend up to 20 years training to become a master of this craft, the craft of the wise.

Manannan Mac Lir, the founder and ruler over the land of immortality, bears a silver apple branch – a wand in the form of a branch, like a little spike or crescent with gently tinkling bells upon it. Music is a special attribute of the fair folk. Their music is heavenly – hence enchantment, and I wonder sometimes about the use of the word enchantment, or enchanting, and its link with music and chanting to take us into a psi-conducive state of consciousness. I feel that sound energy is a vital clue to their magic and to the magic of the stone circles. As in the tale, told in chapter 1, of the Merry Maidens stone circle being created by a faery piper who played such wonderful music that the maidens could not stop dancing, and so became the stone circle. There is a magic to music. Gregorian chant is said to be constructed in such a way as to take us in to trance, and the use of music, drum rhythms in particular, has been used by many a shamanic culture to induce trance, either in the whole community for a ceremony, or just for the shaman. We know very little about the power of sound, yet the Hindus consider sound to be incredibly important for inducing a spiritual state of being, as in their use of mantra, and chanting the sacred texts such as the Ramayana and the Bhagavad Gita.

This sacred branch of the apple tree bearing blossoms or fruit, or sometimes just an apple, is the passport of the otherworld, gifts of the queen of Tir-na-Nog, often serving as food, sometimes making sweet music. Irish druids made their wands of divination from the yew tree. The yew was the Celtic symbol of rebirth. Hawthorn trees are considered to be faery trees and blossom at the old Celtic festival of Beltain (May Day). Could this tree lore have come down from the Neolithic peoples via faery lore? Perhaps this is linked with the traditional witch's broomstick. The broom was a sacred symbol to many early peoples. Originally the broom was the wand, but there is a suggestion by some anthropologists that it was used to anoint certain parts of the body with the flying ointment.

Travelling between the worlds, in its simplest form nowadays is known as the out-of-body experience (OBE). In its most dramatic it is called the near-death experience (NDE), in which the person appears to travel to the otherworld, the world of the dead, there to meet with either loved ones who have died, or with spiritual figures or divinities. Not only are we visited in this world by the denizens of the otherworld but we can travel there in full consciousness ourselves.

OBEs occur spontaneously in about 20% of the population, according to various surveys conducted by parapsychologists, which, if you think about it, is a huge number of people making this a very common experience. In general such an experience occurs only once or twice but some people have it repeatedly and some learn to do it under conscious control. OBEs may occur in any of the following states, which form a continuum from deep relaxation to crisis: lucid dream – hypnagogic – relaxed waking – trance – psychedelic – shamanic – crisis – NDE.

Many OBEs occur whilst the experient is asleep. About half of the reported spontaneous OBEs occur in the calm, relaxed state; the other half occur some form of crisis, such as in childbirth, under anaesthesia, or car accidents. Meditation is said to help one to learn how to go out of body under conscious control, just as it helps us bring psi information into consciousness. This suggests a normal human function dependent on psychological factors.

The classic experience is usually a calming and transcending experience, but many people do experience fear, in that it is such a shock to find yourself out of your body that you immediately return – and then want to get out again! And some say that it was their greatest experience ever.

Many people report that it alleviates the fear of death and encourages belief in after life. For some the OBE is a literal demonstration of personal immortality. Typically it creates a world-view shift, a holistic view of universe, the knowledge that mind exists separate from body.

There are three main types of OBE: asensory in which perceptual like impressions are absent; naturalistic which relate to a familiar environment or what appears to be a normal, earthly realm; and supernaturalistic in which the perceived world is regarded by the person experiencing the OBE to be another plane of existence. This is the shamanic type, the one in which we can shift to the otherworld, and is normally called astral travelling.

The person sometimes finds that their consciousness seems to be within some sort of spatial form, often called the astral body, which is normally felt to be a body of light. Or else you feel yourself to be disembodied, lacking any spatial form, just a point or pure mind.[7]

Paul Devereux[8] has studied this aspect of shamanism in his ley lines research and describes it in his book on shamanism and ley lines. If, in potential, one can astral travel in the true sense of the words, and thus can mentally link with any place in the Universe one chooses, then the awesome potential of the mind is realised and it becomes essential to be careful with one's thoughts, since thoughts not only potentially link with all of creation but can also materialise into physical reality, as mentioned in chapter 2 with regard to the research on OBEs with Keith Harary and Alex Tanous. The Buddhist creed of 'Right Thought' strikes home in a very dramatic and immediate manner. Full activation of our psi potential brings considerable responsibility and a dreadful need for a truly spiritual state of being: a realisation of the divinity within each of us. It is clear that many shamanic cultures have not had a sufficiently moral philosophy or world-view to back up the practices of the shamans, which has led to hex deaths, cursing and all of the other evil practices that our culture traditionally used to assign to witches.

However walking between the worlds is not just the experience of being out of one's body and seeing the world from this perspective – it is the ability to enter the otherworld, the world of death and of divinity. Nowadays such an experience is called a near-death experience (NDE). People who report an NDE frequently comment on the ineffability of the experience, of the feelings of bliss, peace and quiet, light and love. The core experience is that of going into a dark tunnel or some other transition, rather like Cormac going into the mist of a timeless perception; meeting others who have already died and often a Being of Light, our modern equivalent of Manannan Mac Lir. The Being of Light is not of any particular religion, you will see according to your cultural conception. There may be some sort of review, and there is normally a paradisiacal environment, including such things a music, flowers, cities of light, etc., and a yearning to stay there forever. In other words, a classic otherworld faery experience.

People report that NDEs tend to have dramatic after effects on their lives, as with Cormac being given the magical cup of truth. The NDE[9] can be a catalyst for a spiritual awakening, which encompasses a sense of total acceptance and forgiveness; a sense of homecoming; communication with light, which imparts knowledge of universal nature and enables one to see one's life in new way, so that it is clear what truly matters in life.

These transcendental hallucinations are a personal experience of divinity – not belief, but experience. Like in the ancient Mystery Traditions, death = god = love. What I love about this is that the Western medical technology is based on a totally materialistic view of life. The doctors who practise the resuscitation techniques, which have allowed so many people in the West to have this profound mystical experience, are for the most part completely unaware of the spiritual implications of what they are doing. It is just the same as what has happened in physics. There we have probed matter to the point where it has turned into the mystical quantum world. As Sir James Jeans said, 'Mind no longer appears as an accidental intruder into the realm of matter; we are beginning to suspect that we ought to hail it as the creator and governor of the realm of matter'[10] And our medical technology, that treats the body like a machine with its component parts, is now giving people the greatest spiritual initiation experience that one can have – to travel to the otherworld and back in full consciousness.

The personality changes that occur as a result of this experience include the following value changes or changes in self concept, what Maslow[11] has called 'self actualization'. This includes such things as tolerance for others, religious feelings, ability to express love openly, desire for solitude, appreciation of life, concern for others and less concern with impressing others, less materialism, a quest for meaning, a tendency to characterise oneself as spiritual rather than religious, a feeling of being inwardly close to god, a de-emphasis of formal aspects of religious life and worship, a conviction of life after death, openness to reincarnation and Eastern ideas, a belief in an essential underlying unity of all religions and a desire for a universal religion embracing all humanity, psychic development and planetary visions.

This truly is a major initiatory experience, a spiritual awakening, and accounts of such experiences are found in most of the major religious and philosophical books such as the Bible, the Tibetan Book of the Dead, Plato and Swedenborg.

The Otherworld

The otherworld to which one goes when astral travelling or during an NDE, the world of the dead, our ancestors, of divinity and the fair folk, is traditionally located in barrows, knolls, mounds, castles, duns, brughs, sithein (sheean) and raths. Sithein are faery hills of particularly green appearance and rounded form. It is sometimes underground and sometimes over the water to the West, a fair country as bright as day, just like you get in the Pied Piper of Hamelin. It is flat and green without hills and dales. There are castles with crystal battlements, or a cave brilliantly lit. There are apple orchards, crystal streams, beautiful gardens with flowers and birds.

Elfame is surrounded by a wilderness. Woods and forests are also home to the fair folk. The fairyland of Thomas the Rhymer is without sun or moon, with streams of blood and water and the continual sound of the sea, water rushing and clamouring all the time. The Tuatha lived in Tir-na-Nog, an isle in the West, an overseas paradise, a domain which is best described as a land of the gods. At one time it was known by many names. It is also the land of the ancestors, in which they reside in bliss, and to which favoured mortals may be admitted while still alive so that they may share the happiness of the divinities. Peace and plenty are its chief attributes. Plenty of wines and ales, beautiful scenery, the people noble and friendly beyond all human standards, old age unknown, no sickness, flowers everywhere, mead and fresh milk flow, and everyone is on permanent holiday. The Arthurian equivalent is the Isle of Avalon. In Scotland this paradise is called Sorcha, in Wales Annwn, in Cornwall Lyonesse. There is considerable correspondence in descriptions of the two lands, underground and overseas, in all the different strands of faery lore.

Some of the Tuatha live in Ireland in the barrows, raths, etc., and some overseas in Tir-na-Nog. The Irish Sidhe are a race of beings who are like mortals, but are not mortals. Some modern Irish faeries descend in an unbroken line from the ancient pantheon of the Irish gods, the Tuatha de Danaan. Faery Ireland was thick with royalty and a map could be drawn of the various faery kingdoms which is very similar to the mortal divisions. The long barrow, New Grange on River Boyne in Ireland, is strongly associated with the Irish fair folk, the Tuatha de Danaan, built by Neolithic people and the burial place of the High Kings of Tara, the sacred and religious centre of ancient Ireland. You get the same with the Scottish and Welsh fair folk, some living in wild places on this earth and some on the otherworld. There is considerable correspondence in descriptions of the two types of lands, the underground and the overseas. The heaven world of the ancient Celts was not situated in some distant, unknown region of planetary space, but here in another dimension of earth.

In the faery faith, death is less a change of condition than a journey, a departure for another world. Thus, the dead can show themselves to the living; apparitions, phantom funerals and death warnings abound in Celtic lands. Just as psychics can see faeries so can they see the dead. After death the soul still exists and travels amongst us. The banshee, mentioned as the grey lady ghost, the shining one, the being of light in chapter 2, may be a representative of a Celtic goddess of death. This is very common in India where some families have their own personal deity who has been honoured for generations. The lore concerning the ancestors is very similar to that of the faeries: the dead guard hidden treasure; the dead take the living after sunset; can make themselves invisible at will, and disappear at cockcrow. The dead are also said to frequent crossroads, which together with barrows links us back to ley lines and places on the earth where the veil between our material realm and the psychic is very thin.

Another link between the fair folk and our ancestors is the taboo against eating either faery food or food of the dead. As Evans Wentz says: 'Human food is what keeps life going in a human body; faery food is what keeps life going in a faery body; and since what a person eats makes them what they are physically, so eating the food of Faeryland, or of the land of the dead, will make the eater partake of the bodily nature of the beings it nourishes. Hence when a man or woman has once entered into such a relation or communion with the otherworld of the dead, or of faeries, by eating their food, his or her physical body, by a subtle transformation, adjusts itself to the new kind of nourishment, and becomes spiritual like a spirit's or fairy's body, so that the eater cannot re-enter the world of the living'.[12] This compares directly with the Christian communion in which partaking of the body of Christ enables one to enter the kingdom of heaven. This of course is the essential mystery behind prasad for the Hindus, or eating of the sacrificial animals in earlier pagan rites.

To eat of food proffered binds one to the giver, as with any gift or debt, a relationship is formed. The eating of faery food, making one as of faery nature, is part of the ancient belief in the communion with supernatural beings, as mentioned in the tale of Cormac, when he entered Manannan's hall and took part in the feast. Mortals, if they wished, could live in the world of the sidhe for ever. A magical bodily transmutation can occur if one lives in faery land so that on returning one must not touch anything, else one turns to dust, because of the time shift, as, for example, in the tale of Bran and Nechtan. In this tale they thought they had spent but a year and a day in the Land of the Women, but on returning to Ireland, the legends of Bran were very ancient indeed, and Nechtan who left the boat turned to dust on reaching the shore, so Bran told the people about his travels to the Land of the Women from the safety of his boat. This time shift is the same as in the tale of Rip Van Winkle. In another tale where one of the Fianna Faill, a Celtic hero, rode off with a Tuatha lady to Tir-na-Nog, and after a while begged her to be allowed to return. She warned him not to touch the earth and lent him the magic steed. On returning to Ireland, he saw that men had become puny, and a dozen of them were trying to lift a rock that in his time he could have raised with one hand, so he bent down to lift it for them, and the girth broke and he fell to earth and immediately became an ancient, old man. This tale is redolent of the era of the megalithic people and the mystery to later people of how they could have built those fantastically huge monuments.

Pagan Deities

We call our most powerful archetypal experience Deity, or Divinity, or Spirit, or Consciousness, or God, or Goddess. Divinity is the experience of a power that gives and takes life, of a point from which life springs and towards which it aims, and in which the meaning and purpose of creation and our place in it becomes apparent. My feeling is that our deity figures come from a 'universal substrate present in the environment',[13] as Jung calls it. Thus the land called Britain has a certain energy and its specific faery faith lore and mythology. This mythology links us directly to the spiritual energies of this land.

I think that every part of this earth has its archetypal spirit, and by connecting with that spirit so we connect deeper with the land on which we live. This energy of place affects humans in terms of personality. I think that this is behind what we understand by national personalities, for example the so-called feyness of the Celtic peoples, as well as affecting us in terms of our national spiritual identity. Modern Americans seem to be becoming far more 'native' as the generations pass and the spirit of the land of America affects their psyches. By rediscovering the myths of Britain so I reconnect at a deeper level with the spirit (sprite?) of Britain. If you live in America or Canada, or Australia, what are the myths of the land in which you live, both the local myths and the national myths? By learning them, so you will connect with that land in a much deeper way – at the soul level. This is what so many people who have emigrated to new lands are missing – the soul connection with the land, with the spirit of the land. One cannot live on the surface; we need roots for health. This is why so many people are wanting to

Brighde milking her cow, taken from a stone carving on the tower on the top of Glastonbury Tor. (Illustration courtesy of Jill Smith.)

connect with the native peoples and their cultures, so that their souls can grow in harmony with the land on which they are living. We ignore this mythic, archetypal aspect at our peril. I think that the people in the USA have had such profound UFO experiences in the past few decades because their souls were crying out for this reconnection, and they connected with the aerial spirits because they had no links with the earth spirits. This is why living on a sacred site has the effect it has.

One of the Celtic deities who is enjoying a remarkable revival at the moment is St. Brigit, known also as Brighde, whose festival is at Imbolc, the beginning of Spring, on the 1st of February when the first snowdrops appear. She is a remnant of the Divine Mother, Dana, of the Tuatha. She is maiden, as well as midwife to the birthing ewes (Imbolc means ewe's milk), poetess, silversmith, guardian of both wells and of fire. She is both Pagan and Christian, for the 2nd of February is Candlemas when Mary takes her new son (sun) out to the temple after being born at winter solstice. This is the time when the sun starts to noticeably rise higher in the sky, give more warmth and the days lengthen faster and faster until the spring equinox.

Are all our deities archetypes? Do we create our deities according to our need? Are the 'old' deities actually being recast and remoulded according to the needs of this time? Exactly how do we conceive of Brighde, Pan, Cerridwen, Cernunnos, etc. at the moment? I see the mythological seeds of the new spirituality in the feminist goddess and pagan spirituality emerging now. There is not a collective cultural conception. Different people have different feelings, ideas and visions, behind these so-called ancient gods and goddesses; we are making them anew. We might think that we are rediscovering the old British mythology but we must recognise that the way we are conceiving of triple goddess, horned one, Green Man, or whatever are in fact modern conceptions of ancient myths.

Other lands have their own particular energy and therefore their own deities, and yet at a deeper level these are the same as ours, the same in that we all are linking into the spirituality of this planet. And so we are mixing in stuff from the East – Shiva, Ganesh; stuff from Greece, Pan, Pandora; from Rome, all the astrological symbols for the planets use Roman symbology; from American Indians; Aborigines and so on. In fact we seem to be creating a global mythology which has its roots from all over the world and a mongrel mythic tree is in process of growing, a mythology of the whole planet tempered by the spirit of the actual place in which we grow our roots. The Dalai Lama calls this 'The Spiritual Supermarket' – all of the world's great mystery teachings are available for all of us to learn and grow by in this remarkable age.

Myth gives expression to the deeper truth that forms the background to our own personal experience. It is the soil out of which our beliefs, prejudices, attitudes, and in fact our whole way of life, our world-view grows. For me this growth of a new mythology means that the collective unconscious is going through a dramatic growth, and the collective unconscious can be understood as the mind of nature herself. The myth of Atlantis is a classic example of an old myth in a new form appropriate for this age. I see it changing itself almost year by year, a myth of our time telling us of the dangers of our technological culture not respecting the earth who will flood us all if we don't take great care. Just look at the way the Atlantis myth has developed over the centuries since Plato, and see the parallel with the way our technological society has developed.

This has happened before at the end of the last Ice Age and it can certainly happen again. If we get our mythology right, then our belief-systems and our actions will all flow appropriately. So keep questioning the mythology that comes along – keep checking it out – don't just accept it because it's the latest craze, the latest in-thing; look to feel its deepest import and the ethics, morality, life style, world-view that is implied by it. Look at the symbols you use – do you like the mythology attached to them. One of my gripes with modern astrology is that it uses Roman deities and I don't particularly like the mythology associated with Rome, just as what I've heard of Roman civilisation doesn't make me feel too happy about their world-view or life style. Also astrology is still linked to the Age of Aries of 2000 BCE,[14] since it takes the constellation Aries as the rising sign at the Vernal Equinox, when for the past 2000 years it has actually been Pisces and very soon we will move on to Aquarius! So I'm thinking it could be a good idea to change our symbology of the planets – how about Manannan instead of Neptune, or even Rhiannon, and turn this archetype into the feminine which is far more appropriate for the deep unconscious ocean archetype anyway? Get good strong clear deity images and we have models – so let's make sure we get them right! It isn't God who takes clay and makes humans in his own image, it's the other way round.

For this reason I feel great concern at the development of the present UFO mythology. Let's hope that we become mature enough to interact with beings from other dimensions so we can dance in circles with them and learn the art of wisdom from them, rather than the gruesome experiences people are having right now at the turn of the millennium.

One of the aspects about divine beings in all the various myths and legends is that they represent for us archetypal ways of being, lessons in life that we all have to learn in our self-development, our aspirations to be better people, to realise our own divine natures, aspects of life, and our highest ideals as well as failings that we work to overcome. In other words we create our pantheons from our own subconscious fears, imagination, hopes and longings. Thus, divinities of any particular pantheon are a mirror of the peoples who created them. To rediscover our own Celtic and possibly even pre-Celtic, Neolithic, pantheon, gives us an insight into the people who created this pantheon, and returns to us our British culture, rather than the Greek, Roman or Norse culture, with whose pantheons we are most familiar at present.

As each generation passes so does our spirituality evolve. I am beginning to feel that myths of a Golden Age are not about some mythic past but about an ideal future to which we yearn, and towards which we are growing, just as our Atlantis myth is a warning about the dangers inherent in our society now.

I feel very excited by the intensely personal mix and matching of the global spiritual theologies that is occurring at the moment. Each person has their own spiritual beliefs and you just cannot have any more religious wars when every person has their own religion! In looking at and attempting to express the so-called new spirituality, I am taking what I have seen to be popular grass root movements as the very things that are of the most importance because they are emerging from people's real needs, despite ourselves – there is no preconceived structure that we are aiming towards – this is what is actually happening to us.

As with the Greek myths, the Irish gods and goddesses helped the humans in their wars, as well as having wars themselves, in the eternal mythic battle of good against bad. Thus, the battles of Moytura are a record of a long warfare to determine the spiritual control of Ireland by the Tuatha representing gods of all that is good, and the Fomorians, representing gods of that which we must strive against. Humans, such as Cuchulain, Conn, Finn and Cormac, fought in this battle. At one level this is the Celtic patriarchal war god level of myth, and at another level it is a connection with the older pre-Celtic philosophy. The Fates are there in all our lives; they spin and weave in the myths of every land. The three war goddesses often exercise their magical powers under the form of royston crows, in Scotland as hoody-crows, in Brittany as magpie, in Wales as the crow, in Scandinavia and Germany as raven. This connection of the magical with crows extends even so far as the sacred ravens in the Tower of London, and the crow as a special messenger in Tibetan divinatory lore. Connecting with birds as creatures of omen, as with trees and their sacred properties, is an intrinsic part of the growing animism and it is worth being aware of this mythology also.

The Collective Unconscious

When we start to look at deity we look at the archetypal, the mythic, the collective unconscious. This, as far as I am concerned, is the chthonic mind – the consciousness of the planet herself which finds form through our imagination, through our dreaming. The conscious mind is but a small part of our psyche. There is also the subliminal mind which is composed of many aspects, such as the preconscious, which is stuff that you are just aware of but not sufficiently to consciously recognise what is there, as I described in chapter 1. The subliminal mind decides what comes into consciousness, is in charge of our moods, our actions, our thoughts. And this is only the first level of the unconscious – that which decides the contents of our awareness is composed of all the stuff which has come in during our life, our personal unconscious, all the stuff from our family, from our village, or town, our tribe, our culture, our society. All of this stuff makes up who we are and how we behave and how we react to situations, and it is all totally unconscious. At each level we broaden our connection with the world around us – the personal is just us, the family we hold in common with our family; the tribe we hold in common with a broader range of people, say all working class people in a particular county; the social we feel a commonality with all people of our caste or class; the national, all Welsh, or Scots; the cultural, all Western English speakers, until we reach the collective unconscious which is held in common by all humanity, which has no bar of culture, or race or language.

If I were to tell you the tale of Inanna, the queen of heaven who had to go to the underworld, and in doing so had to cast aside her seven veils so that she arrived there naked, to be faced with her sister Ereshkigal, queen of the underworld, who hung her up on a hook like a piece of meat and from which she was rescued, I would be telling you a tale that is as alive today as it was 6000 years ago in Babylon when it first found form. Because this is a tale of the soul's journey – the descent to the underworld is a journey we all make at some point in life, whether in childhood from abuse, or later from bereavement and grief, and some point we go down there and are naked in the pit. It is a great initiation into soul growing. This is an archetypal myth and it doesn't matter what your culture, you resonate with it.

Reincarnation

Reincarnation is another aspect of the faery faith which is once again coming into popular belief. The essential belief is that the soul persists after the death of one body and at some time becomes associated with a new body. The essential philosophy of reincarnation is that nothing dies; all things evolve cyclically in such a way that at every cycle they are renewed and improved. All things must change is the universal law.

Belief in reincarnation has occurred independently in different places and at different times. Egyptians, Indians, Greeks, Romans, Celts and many other nations have all taught a reincarnation doctrine of some form. In the Mystery schools, it formed the cornerstone of the most important philosophical systems like those of Buddha, Pythagoras, Plato, the Neo-Platonists, and the Druids. In fact, of all the major religions the Christian and Moslem seem unusual in not having a re-incarnation doctrine. For Christianity, this occurred in 550 AD at the 2nd Council of Constantinople, when Origen and the early Christian 'fathers' outlawed reincarnation in Christian theology.

The Irish heroes were avatars or reincarnations of the early gods, i.e. related to the Tuatha de Danaan. For example the goddess Eatin becomes the mortal wife of the Irish king Conchobar. Dechtire, his sister and mother of Cuchulain, is called a goddess. Cuchulain is an avatar of Lugh, a sun deity, literally the god of light. For example, Conn entered a rath and beheld Lugh seated beside a woman of great beauty, described as the Sovereignty of Erinn till the day of doom. She married Lugh at the annual feast of Lughnassad. 'The earthly monarch of Ireland typified this god Lugh; he was his worldly representative, and he was ritually married to this goddess or to a woman symbolising her at the time of his coronation'.

There are many different philosophies surrounding the belief in reincarnation. Some believe, like the Druses of Lebanon, in instant reincarnation, that as soon as you die you reincarnate, sometimes even into a foetus that is already several months old. The Jains also believe in instant reincarnation. But with them you reincarnate at conception. Some believe that you may spend many years in other realms, e.g. the Hindus and Buddhists have no fixed death–rebirth interval. Some believe you may hang around this earth for a while and some that we only have one life and never reincarnate. People having experiences linked with reincarnation have been found in every culture where the belief is strong, and in some where it is not.

There has been some research into this in parapsychology, notably by Ian Stevenson.[15] Stevenson started research in 1961. By 2001 he had collected over 2000 cases of children who remembered a previous life. 80% were investigated to some extent. These children, at the age of 2–3 years, start to talk about memories of a previous life. They will name relatives such as a husband or wife, children they may have had, brothers and sisters. They will also talk about the place where they lived, the sort of work they used to do, and most particularly the manner in which they died. They will normally talk a lot about this death and the events preceding it. There is a high frequency of sudden death in the previous life, either murder, accident or illness. They normally forget these memories by about 5–7 years of age.

They also show unexpected behaviour linked with the previous personality that they are remembering, e.g. phobias or special interests. The social strata of the previous person and the child are often widely differing, which can cause considerable problems both for the child and the family in which they have been born. Another problem can be caused by the child showing 'adult' attitudes and behaviour. They often ask to be taken to the place where they lived before and show concern over the people 'left behind'. Sometimes, although relatively rarely, they will have a birthmark or deformity that is related to the previous life, or they may even have a disease related to the previous life.[16] And occasionally the pregnant mother, or a relative, may have an 'announcing dream' in which the deceased personality indicates to the dreamer the intention to reincarnate.

There are also considerable cultural differences. For example, violent death occurs in 38% of the Sri Lankan cases and in 78% of the

Druses. Some cultures believe that you will always be reborn the same sex as the previous person, e.g. the Alevis or Druses, but most have opposite sex rebirth in 55% of the cases, whilst in Burma and Thailand, only 20% are opposite sex. So this is definitely related to cultural belief.

In most cases the child and the previous person are closely related and live within 15 miles, which is a very close association. There are some international cases, but these in general seem to be much weaker. Also the death rebirth interval is normally from 9 months to 2 years on average, which is a remarkably short time period.

In general, children who remember a previous life almost always remember a life that ended very shortly before theirs started, and nearly always it was a life that was cut short dramatically through murder, or illness or accident. They also lived very close by in the previous life. Because of these facts I think that these cases are a very special form of reincarnation in which the soul, spirit, or whatever it is that survives physical death, never really leaves this plane of existence and incarnates very quickly into a new conception bringing the whole personality and ego with it. How quickly, and whether or not it is an already conceived foetus, depends on the belief system of the culture. The fact that these cases are so influenced by the belief system supports my feeling that they are a very special case, and not a general typical form of reincarnation. There are relatively few people who as children remember a previous life, who have birthmarks or personality character-istics that are clearly related to a previous personality. Most of us seem to leave the ego and personality characteristics of any possible previous life behind, and start afresh with each new life.

Rebirth and the Holographic Universe

I want to try to give an overview of ideas concerning reincarnation by looking at all the data from parapsychology. I shall start with that concerning OBEs and NDEs, which suggest that there is something that leaves and can persist independently of the body. The second aspect of para-psychology to touch on this topic is that of ghosts and apparitions. In general, ghosts who interact with people, giving a message or smiling or whatever, are ghosts of people who are recently deceased. It is quite rare to have an interactive apparition when the person has died 50 years or more before. Ghosts, hauntings and apparitions of this long term sort tend to be of the repetitive type where the same movements or actions occur and they stare through people who encounter them or walk past with no recog-nition. The same thing occurs with mediums. In general when they bring messages through from people who have died it is for the recently bereaved that they give messages. So there seems to be a cut-off point when com-munication between this world and the otherworld ceases – which is approximately one to two generations, about 50 years on average. Interestingly, the other source of reincarnation data, that of hypnotic regression, tends to feature people who remember lives which are in general at least 100 years previous to their present life. This is in complete contrast to the children who remember a previous life. So it seems as if memories, personality, ego are maintained for a certain period and then the soul or spirit no longer exists in a form which can communicate with this world.

One aspect of all these phenomena is that when they manifest physi-cally they do so in a way that something can occasionally be captured on film, a light sort of something like ectoplasm, and which can maybe affect psychics so that they are aware of the OBE person, or the ghost or apparition, and which perhaps can affect matter as we get in psycho-kinesis. In other words, there seems to be something in the idea of an energy body of some sort. Mediums create ectoplasm which seems to be the same sort of semi-physical, semi-psychic substance. This substance of OBEs, of BVM apparitions, of ghosts, apparitions, hauntings and poltergeists can affect matter.

The world view I call the holographic universe, which I described in chapter 2, physicist David Bohm[17] calls 'the implicate order', because it is that level which stands behind (and is therefore implied by) this manifest physical, see–touch, time and space level we inhabit. This light aspect of reality, this quantum reality, exhibits the strange property called quantum entanglement, which means that all knowledge is there and each part connects with all other parts at this level. He describes it by asking you to imagine a jar of glycerine in which a spot of ink has been dropped. If you stir this glycerine, the spot of ink will gradually get spread out to the point where it becomes totally invisible, inter-mingled with the glycerine. If you then stir it an equal number of times in the opposite direction, it reforms into the spot of ink once again. So when it was invisible it was still there, but only in the implied, or implicate, state, and when stirred back it became explicate again and you could see it. It was there all the time it just changed the way it which it manifested, either one enfolded into the whole of the glycerine, or an individual spot manifested out. 'Ordinarily we think of each point of space and time as distinct and separate, and that all rela-tionships are between contiguous points in space and time. In the enfolded order we see, first of all, that when the droplet is enfolded it is in the WHOLE thing, and every part of the whole thing contributes to the droplet. When two droplets are present they are in different positions in the explicit state, but when they are enfolded they are distributed through the whole and are interspersed, interpenetrated with each other. In the enfolded order every element has direct connections with each other – even with distant elements'. It is out of this implicate level that we manifest. Bohm uses the word explicate, the opposite of implicate, and calls this see–touch world we inhabit the explicate order.

So in principle all parts are omniscient. In principle, all that has been is or will be, is present in the eternal now of this implicate level. Bohm suggests that this see–touch reality we live in is a secondary reality, which arises out of the primary, the implicate order, in which everything is interconnected. Bohm's implicate order has many characteristics in common with the magical, spiritual world view.

This gives us an interesting slant on reincarnation ideas. When you look at mediums' transcripts, in which they are perhaps picking up on the spirit of someone who has died, you find that in general the person who they channel is fairly recently dead. It is much rarer for there to be a spirit who died thirty of forty years ago, much more common for it to be someone who has died in the previous four or five years. People who have NDEs talk about going to a place where there is a being of light, where they meet with people who they know who have died. Is there maybe a sort of halfway house, where we go when recently dead, in which we can still have some sort of communication with the earth and the people upon her. When you look at hypnotic regression, most people remember a previous life that was some distance in the past, 100 or 200 years ago. Very rarely do they mention a life that was only a few years before their previous one started. So it seems as though those of us who don't remember our life before, have had an intervening existence in some other form. But there is no evidence for this other than hypnotic regression, which is a remarkably uncertain form of evidence.

There is a suggestion that we can think of rebirth in another way – that the soul that incarnates as you or me is a unique soul. This soul is part of the whole, as in the holographic theory, and so contains the whole from its unique perspective. Its particular perspective will have stronger resonance with some aspects of the whole and less resonance with other aspects. So, when hypnotised, you may remember a life as, for example, a soldier in the Crimea war. This does not necessarily mean that you were that soldier, just that you, in your unique aspect of the whole, have a strong resonance with this, and you remember details perfectly correctly through what is called super ESP, or in theosophical terms, connecting with the Akashic record. In theory, through psi we can know everything in the whole universe, we are potentially omniscient. Through the holographic theory we, at one level, are one, the whole. And linking to this level we know everything and can manifest, or explicate, what is relevant to now. So each incarnation is unique and each incarnation in its life affects the whole, which thereby affects each new incarnation.

There is a lovely Sufi teaching story which is relevant here:

There was a stream running down from the mountains and it came to a desert into which is sank. The stream very much wanted to cross the desert, but try as it might it just sank into the sand. The sand heard its longing and said, 'Why don't you let wind carry you across the desert'. 'No', said the stream, 'because then I would no longer be me, the stream. I would be lost into wind'. But time passed and the stream kept on sinking into the sand, and the sand kept on suggesting that the wind crossed the desert, and the stream was just becoming a rather nasty, smelly, stagnant pool of water. So, one day the stream let go, let go into the wind, became air, and with the wind crossed the desert. On the other side of the desert there were mountains, and as the wind lifted up over the mountains and cooled, so the water that had been stream condensed out and fell as rain, and in time became part of another stream flowing down those mountains.

There are many, many forms of belief concerning reincarnation. I like this form because it is totally non-selfish. I am a unique soul. I have resonance with aspects of this earth that feel like memories and are great teachings for me to work with in this life, and I understand these memory-like feelings as my particular strong resonances within the whole. Through knowing that every thought, feeling and action that I make is affecting the whole, that my life affects the whole for good or for bad, that when I die and once again become part of the whole, that any future incarnations will be affected by what I have become in this life, so my aim to grow to become a beautiful, loving soul that does good is not just a personal growth, but a growth for the good of the whole.

Linked with this philosophy in reincarnation, and nowadays returning to the West in rather garbled form, is a belief in karma: that certain afflictions in this life can be penalties for sins committed in a former life. While it is wise to be wary of most New Age beliefs concerning karma, because this can lead to a sort of fascism, it should always be borne in mind as a possibility because there are certain instances where a person's congenital disabilities or pattern of life experience can be best understood in a rebirth context. But it is only in children who remember previous lives that we can clearly see that their disability was clearly linked with that previous life. I prefer the boddisattva view of karma, that every thought, word and action that I make reverberates throughout the whole universe. This is the Holographic Universe philosophy, and for sure it means that by affecting the whole so the unique souls that are yet to be born will be affected, just as I am affected because the whole is present in every part, and so is affected by every part. But it does not lead to the fascistic sort of philosophy, which says that you chose to be born into this particular circumstance, and so you are responsible for all your ills from the bad you did in a previous life. No, it accepts that the universe is the way it is, that there are social and cultural ills which can hurt a person through no fault of that person; and that we all need to address ourselves to healing this planet of the ills which beset her through humanity's doing.

It was Heathcote Williams, in his play 'The Immortalist',[18] about longevity, which first led me to deeply consider the manner in which most people are conceived, though I have always been concerned with what I call conscious conception. If one is a very aware, loving person and you decide you want to have a child, then what I did was I stopped taking contraception, let my cycle normalise, and then consciously worked out when I would be fertile and made the sexual act that day be a very special one, a conscious conception of the highest degree possible that I was able to manifest. My children were chosen and called into my body clearly. I know the moment for each one, the feeling of a shining spirit entering me. If every person on this planet were consciously conceived in this way, what a difference it would make.

For this is the way that high spirits are brought to this earth plane, and we desperately need high spirits now.

5

Living a Magical Reality: The Folklore of the Faery in Everyday Life

In this chapter, I shall go deeper into the living practice of the old pagan religion of these isles, which became scapegoated and denigrated as witchcraft, particularly its modern mythology and modern form in which its revival is occurring. Old signs of this pagan religion are still to be found in churches with their Sheila-na-Gigs over the door and Green Men on the church bosses.

I consider that the legends of the people who built the megaliths, and their magical society, are the ancient forerunner of the pagan religion of these lands, which was finally ousted by Christianity during the times of the witch trials in the 17th century, merely 300 years ago, and which is returning now in a new form. This was an Earth Magic religion of a people intimately linked with the earth and aware of the energies of the different places and how to use these energies psychically – magically. For our growth into the new we have to let our roots grow deep down. That is the problem with so many Americans. Because they denied the ancient history of their land, the thousands of years of Indian culture, so they stopped themselves from having any roots that could grow deep. As someone said to me once, it is a bit like they have covered the whole land with a layer of concrete and then put a few inches of earth on top of it and they are trying to grow in those few inches of earth. It just doesn't work. And that is why so many young Americans are now looking towards Celtic Witchcraft or to Amerindian shamanic philosophy for their spirituality.

There are many strands in the lore about the fair folk that suggest we are hearing a memory of people who lived in these lands from the end of the Ice Age, 10,000 years ago, until the coming of the Bronze Age Celts. As they had lived many thousands of years in Britain, they were the teachers to the incoming Celts of the local herb lore, of agriculture, the weavers, wearers of green, the dyers, the musicians and dancers. It is

111

this aspect of faery lore, which I link with the old pagan religion of these lands, which is enjoying a resurgence now. It is not the Druid religion of the Celts, but what I see as an older animistic shamanic spirituality, linked to the daemonic spirit reality of the land.

The most obvious link between the fair folk and the old religion is to be found in the witch trials. For example, Donald MacMichael who was tried for sorcery in 1677 at Inverary said that he consorted with the Faery King who was of human stature. Bessie Dunlop, an Ayrshire witch tried in 1576, was visited by a faery queen. Andro Man tried at Aberdeen in 1597 said he had been husband to a faery queen and had children by her. These are the people whose heritage the modern neo-pagans claim.

The Elvish Community: Memories, Myths and Legends of the Neolithic Peoples

The aspect of the myths and legends of the faeries that links most strongly with the Neolithic people is that of the elves. Elves were always believed to dwell in communities. The elf was known throughout Britain and tales about them vary only slightly from area to area. Like all the fair folk they are magic, but they are also neighbourly. However, they are resentful of human interference and must be treated with courtesy or else! Most of the elven folk live in wild places, woods and forests, or in the otherworld.

Perhaps the most telling aspect of this elven lore is that they hated iron; this is a dislike shared by ghosts and other spirits in many parts of the world. If a man fixed his dirk, a dagger or knife, in the door of a faery mound it could not be closed. Infants could be protected from the faery kidnappers by iron in the crib. The Neolithic peoples did not use iron, so in time iron came to be religiously regarded as efficacious against spirits and faeries. More though, the philosophy underlying the magical properties attributed to iron is based on mystical conceptions of virtues attributed to various metals. I think that the following ideas are worth thinking about: Iron is the most strongly magnetic metal. The faeries were said to direct the magnetic currents in the earth according to Evans Wentz. Iron affects our sensitivity to these stronger than any other metal, so if one is working psychically and utilising the GMF, as talked about in the first chapter, then one's sensitivity would be strongly affected by iron in the vicinity. In understanding the electromagnetic energies of sacred hills, stone circles, etc., and of our own bodies, so we begin to realise how strongly iron affects us and our environment physically and psychically. It is not just our electric society in which we are never more than a few miles away from an electricity cable of some sort that is affecting us at every level, but our ubiquitous use of iron.

Wood elves. (Illustration courtesy of Brian Froud. Reproduced from Faeries *by Brian Froud and Alan Lee, Pan Books, 1979.)*

The elven folk are also skilled in crafts. As spinners and dyers the elfin women were unrivalled, thus resembling the Fates of classical mythology. Fair folk wear green; or fawn skins; or graceful linen garb of black, grey, green or white; or red, blue and green; or green with a red or blue cap with a feather. In faery lore, green symbolises eternal youth, resurrection or rebirth as in nature during spring time. Thus in the initiation ceremonies, on return to the physical plane after the trance the initiates were dressed in green, for they had penetrated the Mystery of Death. Green symbolises the birth of the world and the moral creation or resurrection of the initiate. Many mythic peoples have green especially attributed to them; Melwas had a green cloak, Robin Hood and Maid Marian dressed in green. Gwenhywvar tells her knights to dress in green, and in one tale had a green horse. This symbolism concerning green is found in other times and places as well. In the evergreen the Master Mason finds the emblem of hope and immortality.

Knowing this about the symbolism of green and the fair folk, makes the Green Movement even more appropriately named, for it is the physical aspect of the neo-pagan spiritual movement to honour and love and cherish and care for the earth, and the fair folk are the beings of the earth.

Hunting and riding in procession are the most commonly reported activities of the faery court, riding by moonlight with jingling of silver bells along the faery paths, which can be linked with ley lines. Faery horses are milk white in hue. This belief is linked with the Wild Hunt; the gods, the supernaturals are the ultimate providers of food, and were seen as the controllers of the game supply, and they themselves hunted it down. The Sluagh of the West Highlands were actually thought of as hunting men with bows and arrows during their flight through the air, so that they might capture souls. The Sluagh are sometimes regarded as faeries, at others as the dead, this link between fair folk, ancestors and divinity being inextricably intertwined. This Wild Hunt is also seen as the energy of death – the grim reaper which takes us into the otherworld. Gwynn ap Nudd rides with his white hounds who have red ears and red eyes.

Morality

The elves appear as a moral force; they are invariably on the side of justice. The faery faith recognises an intimate relationship between humans and nature; the fair folk as the animate intelligent aspect of the natural world around us guides every act of human life. As long as people keep themselves in harmony with this unseen faery world in the background of nature, all is well. In all parts of Britain, at one time it was considered essential to keep on good terms with the fair folk. They were good neighbours, but relentless enemies, as mentioned in the polter-geist chapter. This idea comes from the belief that faery folk, in their aspect of gods, personify the sense of justice and right dealing. This aspect of religion is vital to our human growth, we need a moral and ethical superstructure to guide us, and this the faery faith provides. Their code is akin to all religious spiritual paths. It does not separate religious ritual practice from everyday life, so every facet of life is imbued with religious significance.

In the faery philosophy, the faeries, as powers of life, the type of karmic philosophy I have just been talking about, organise ordinary living and the ritual of life. Vice and greed are invariably punished – the lore of enough becomes the creed; the deserving poor take the places of the rich, what I call the dumpies (the downwardly mobile) becomes that which one aims for; 'living lightly on the land', or as the

The Green Man from Roslin chapel, a wonderfully wicked green man image. (Photograph courtesy of Clive Hicks. Reproduced from Green Man *by William Anderson, Compass Books, 1990/2002.)*

slogan says 'live simply so that others may simply live'; the plain but virtuous become the beautiful. This is the 'green' aspect of our spirituality. Every single one of us has to change our way of life in very practical ways. Every action must be done with consideration of this planet uppermost in our minds, and it's probably linked with the dire state of this planet at the moment that this sort of spirituality is emerging so strongly at this time. We must not be complacent in the slightest degree; being Aquarian means being adult, means being responsible for the planet on which we live.

We are wrecking the natural world – not just in tropical lands with the plunder of the rainforests and driving countless thousands of species into extinction but also in the temperate lands where this plunder happened long ago, and now we are destroying the actual landscape itself, by carving through hills just to make a flatter road, building houses over huge areas just so that people can have isolated lives, each living in their own house rather than sharing with others, and all the other symptoms of modern life.

This has all been said before and more eloquently than I can aspire to, but the only way in which we change our lifestyle is by first changing our philosophy, our faith, our world-view, that in which we believe. Our lifestyle is composed of deep, deep habits that we acquired as children from our parents, and then later those we adopted during our late teens and early twenties from our peers and the social pressures at that period of our life. To shift this pattern requires deep resolve. I know people who profess to be 'green' and who use cars, which are the major polluter and resource consumer at present in the world. I have just spent 6 months in India, the first visit there in 25 years. Indian cities are suffering a huge pollution problem, because they have a lifestyle which uses rickshaws. 25 years ago all those rickshaws were bicycles run on human power. Now they are scooters which give out huge clouds of black smoke. In Pune there is a meteorological office which measures the particles in the air. The health limit is 50. When I was there, the count was always over 200, apart from once when it was 193. And Pune is not as bad as Calcutta. The one city that was better was Bombay, which has banned rickshaws from the centre. This is a change that has occurred in the past 25 years. In the west we have clogged our whole land with this pollution, not just the cities. Flying in to Heathrow there was a brown fug all the way up to 800 metres and this covered the whole of the south of England. How often do you see the sun setting in to the horizon these days? Normally now it sets into a brown, misty, foggy zone which stretches some distance above the horizon. We suffer from noise pollution, air pollution, and consumption of material resources to an unsustainable level – and even those people who believe in caring for the earth, who love this planet, find that in our present day culture they cannot live without their cars, and do not want to. They have to shop in the local supermarket even though this supports a culture of plastic waste, of genetically engineered foods and other life destroying substances. So how do we shift our lifestyle? Most people will change their lifestyle at a time of crisis, but how can we bring about a voluntary change without crisis? This seems to be so hard for us. We no longer have the moral force of the faery faith, nor of the Christian faith – somehow we have to fill the gap to help us live according to the sustainable code, that is both morally and ethically good for our souls, and is what the earth requires for healthy survival.

Taboo

In the faery code, as soon as taboo is broken, disharmony sets in. This is what has happened in Western civilisation in particular, and all parts of the world which have been touched by industrialisation. There is a lack of harmony between us and nature which results in physical sickness such as cancer, in stress, in emotional and mental problems, such as the breakdown in relationships which has reached a huge proportion in the West, and is now beginning to occur in the East. It is really interesting to be writing this in India where family is still so very important, where the first question that people ask is about one's family, where everyone lives in close family communities. No one lives alone – it is considered a tragedy to be alone. In the West we have the opposite: many, many people are suffering hugely from their inability to share a house with another person. In the West our individuality, our aloneness, our separation from one another has reached the ultimate – one person to a house.

The whole background of taboo appears to rest on a supernatural relationship between humans and the otherworld. Almost all taboos ought to be interpreted psychologically, or even psychically, and not as ordinary social regulations. We have broken with nature, we have lost contact with the essential spirit of the world, and so we feel dispossessed. And so our contact with spirit materialises as UFO contact, where people have terrifying experiences of abduction, rape and other invasions. When we ignore spirit it manifests as psychosis. My research into the pineal gland suggests that there is a continuum. I have already mentioned how the pineal makes the endogenous equivalent of the shamanic brew ayahuasca, and this is thought to be the chemical trigger for the dream state. The dream state of mind is a link to that state of mind which is the mythical, the archetypal in which we can connect with very deep layers of psyche and the psychedelic experience. If you do not sleep for five days then you will start dreaming whilst awake. When the dream mechanism goes awry you may experience a psychotic breakdown in which you lose touch with everyday reality. In a shamanic culture this may be seen as a shamanic initiation experience. The brain mechanism seems to be very similar – it is just different aspects of the same continuum: dream, psychedelic, shamanic to psychosis. Stepping in to the otherworld in this way can be seen as a spiritual emergence, or in an untrained mind it can be an experience of hell, a fearful frightening experience. We no longer have the shamans who are trained to walk between the worlds, we are no longer in contact with the daemonic, with the spiritual aspects of our world and so we get lost, and end up in mental hospital.

Taboo is also about awe and fear. This fear in the animistic spiritual knowledge, is the knowledge that a great power is over and above the mortal's own needs and wishes, and that sometimes the mortal has to submit to the higher forces. Witches are part of our folk lore and are portrayed as nasty black things that'll get you if you aren't good, and may get you even if you are good, or lay down your fate when you

Witches dancing round a very devilish Pan, or Robin Goodfellow, from a broadsheet of 1628. They look almost identical to the picture of faeries dancing (see Ch.1) in terms of their clothing, illustrating how, in the 1600s, people saw witches and faeries in a similar light. (Reproduced from "Clutching at Straws" by R.J. Rickard in The Crop Circle Enigma, *ed. Ralph Noyes, Gateway Books, 1991.)*

are born – in other words they are seen as a moral force, very similar to the faery lore!!

Both witches and fair folk were feared for their powers to harm you; with fair folk that harm only came if you infringed one of their lores; with the shaman, sorcerer or witch it was called hexing, causing harm to another through magic. Psychic ability is neutral – as with all things it can be used for good or for bad. This is where the fear of the psychic, the fear of magic arises. I often wonder about the witch hunts of the middle ages. In the 1300s there was the Black Death. This was a time of unimaginable horror, in which one third of the population of Europe died. Just think of your family and friends and then count how many would die, and start to try to feel the horror of this. Now in the 1300s the healers were the wise women and cunning men in the villages and towns. They used herbs and traditional lores and were highly respected. These are the people who came to be called witches. They were unable to mitigate the effects of the Black Death, and I can understand how people would come to blame them. They were respected and feared for their knowledge and power, and they were unable to do anything to prevent that great horror. When people are held in awe and they cannot help, then the awe changes to anger and hatred. This occurred around the time of the beginning of the Inquisition by the Roman Catholic Church, who built an enormous number of churches on the ancient sacred sites in Britain at this time. When the Plague struck again in the 1600s that was just too much and so the witch hunts reached their peak. I have often wondered why there was such vehemence by the Puritans against the old healer women and this explanation, to me, gives a good understanding.

So we see here in the two great tragedies of the Black Death and the Plague, together with the Inquisition, a reason for the present day fear of the psychic, and the denial that psychic powers exist. Over a period of several hundred years, magic – that is 'miracles' performed by people who were not recognised holy people of the Catholic church – came to be considered more and more evil, and its practitioners were subjected to the most horrific torture and death if caught. So they became more and more silent about their gifts and training – they went underground. Remember this was a very gradual process over a period of several hundred years. In time nobody ever spoke about magical powers, except as a jeer. And finally people forgot that there had been those with the knowledge and skill, and so anything psychic became 'occult', or hidden, occluded from the sight of society, and finally, in the Age of Reason, it was denied that human beings could possess and use talents that had the hallmarks of divinity about them – especially once a time had been reached when even divinity had been reasoned out of existence.

There is a psychologist called Charles Tart[1] who considers that much of the reason for the 'elusiveness' of psi in the laboratory, and for the incredibly small psi effects seen, is that we are all subconsciously afraid of psi. With such a common history of centuries of persecution for having psychic abilities, followed by centuries of jeering, is it any wonder that people are afraid of psi!

Linked with this lore concerning the moral code is the tradition of the friendly faery. If one assists a fay, often in the guise of old woman etc., then you will receive aid when you most need it, e.g. Cinderella, the Red Etin. This is essentially the law of dana, the first of the Bodhisattva paramitas, doing good gifting with no thought of return, putting out good energy into the world brings its own return often in magical unexpected ways. And as a part of the universe, and as every part contains the whole, so what I put out will become part of me as of everything else. Fair folk used to gift people with good qualities or material treasures, caps or cloaks that make one invisible, chests that hold an inexhaustible supply of grain, excellence in ones craft (Shoemaker and the Elves), boots that make you swift of foot, magic stones which transport you where you will, or super milking powers of cows. These are concrete archetypal images, and nowadays we understand them in more abstract ways; the psychological change in attitude from doing good, which the universe rewards synchronistically by bringing to you just what you need as you need it, so you always have enough, you are always able to get to the places you need to go, etc. It is an attitude to life which gives all and knows that one is held and supported by the universe, and that one's needs will be met.

Ethics and Bad Magic

In my earlier book, *Where Science and Magic Meet*,[2] I used the term 'black' magician to mean what our culture understands by someone who is using magic for evil ends. I was told off severely for linking the concept 'black' with evil. I have taken this criticism on board. I still want to address the same issue of 'black and white' magic and here I use the terms bad and good.

   To do, or to be, bad is a state of mind or personality. The basic principle behind bad magic has been, is, and always will be the same; the use of the power of mind to gain illicitly something one has no right to possess and which causes harm to others. In any person who uses psychic power for bad ends, there is a fantastic egotism, a form of paranoia (the grandiose sort), which stops at nothing in order to satisfy itself. We shall never get rid of bad magic and its 'sins of the mindless' until the sickness within the human psyche, which is its source, is healed.

   Quite possibly the worst magicians of our time are those scientists and intellectuals who deny that there is 'godness' in the world, that there is 'spirit' in a tree, a brook, in a person. Those behaviourist psychologists who were so mindless that they tried to say we were 'stimulus–response' machines, feeling and thinking nothing – without a soul, without any spirit – were unwittingly causing great harm. To the extent that they realised the harm they were doing they were profaning the 'good' within humanity. This is bad magic and it has created a materialist age that is literally murdering the planet and all upon her through avarice, greed, endless consumption of everything including spirituality. Even yoga, a spiritual way of life, is marketed in America as a consumer item. The people who are polluting the air and the seas and threatening the whole planet with destruction must find their souls, their hearts, their spiritual being. At present they are soulless automatons, heartless creatures, to so destroy our beautiful planet. The blackest magicians of our society at present are those who are destroying our planet in the name of their religion of progress and profit (greed and avarice it used to be called). Throwing out the ideal of the visionary and mystical, which is our highest ideal, has led us to the darkest hour of our planet. For we need a highest ideal, we need a conception of the highest good possible, so that we have something to aim for, because what good is an ideal if one does not constantly aim for it. And those who deny any godness in this world, or any spirit, or any soul are thereby speaking out for the forces of evil and darkness, and the material wilderness in which we are lost at this moment.

Anyone can be bad. There are more bad scientists, politicians, military personnel, police, industrialists, farmers, etc., than there are bad occultists. Witness the crazy escalation of armaments, the billions of dollars, pounds, roubles, and every other currency poured into the manufacture of weapons of increasing destructiveness and horror. This is bad magic of the most disgusting and awful form – and we are surrounded by it everywhere we turn.

Like any power psi can be used for good or bad – that depends on the person. And the person who embarks on a training for the enhancement of their psi faculties must be very well developed spiritually. They must have their emotions well controlled. It is well known how powerful human emotions are, and if these find expression psychically there can be disastrous consequences. Poltergeist cases, especially where the focus is an adolescent, are very good examples of the havoc wreaked by undisciplined psychic forces issuing from an emotionally unstable person. The person must therefore develop spiritually to the point where they rid themselves of anger, hate, fear, jealousy, greed, lust, spite, envy, malice, aggression, violence, and all the other negative traits to which so many human beings fall prey. This is why the Eastern disciplines stress so strongly the importance of the spiritual aim – to become one with God and the unimportance of the psychic abilities which are attained along the way. If a person is to train in magic he or she must be true to his or her own self-development first and foremost. I found when I was doing practical experimental work for my postgraduate degree in parapsychology that the participants and I were all undergoing intense personal development – if we were open to that possibility. The actual psi score was merely a milestone marker along this path.

There has been a divorce between magic and religion: magic has been seen to be bad, evil, and those who practise it have been called occultists. This word been used as a stigma. The rebirth of magic is at least partially being fostered by its increasing recognition by science. The findings with regard to psi by parapsychologists is actually speeding up the present interest in the occult, so we must be very careful and must not divorce the magic from religion – religion in the sense of spiritual discipline as in the NDE, 'the enlightenment effect.' We must remember the teachings of Christ, who, after all, was one of the world's greatest well-known magicians, that faith is all important to work miracles. The witches emphasise that magic must never be used to hurt or harm, and only for what is really necessary. The Wiccan Rede, i.e., Counsel or advice of the Wise Ones is: '*An ye harm no one, do what ye will.*' They further state that if you do harm, that it will be returned to you thricefold, which cannot be a bad belief to have whether or not it is true!

Basically all paranormal phenomena have the same source whatever label is put on them – the use of a subtle force to modify matter or conditions. According to witchcraft, the spoken word too has power, so long as the power is not dissipated by idle chatter or lying, so long as it is spoken with meaning, and that an intention once uttered is carried out and the promise fulfilled. This is a good general practice anyway. Therefore we should all learn to watch not only our words, but also our thoughts, as the Buddhist scriptures counsel. Like any other power magic must be treated with respect and care. The necessity of saying this is in itself a symptom of a modern problem.

Connection with the Old Religion: Philosophy of the Faery Faith

In psychical research we go out ghost hunting, or investigate poltergeists, or take people into a laboratory in order to explore the various parameters of how we pick up psychic information, or affect the world through psychic means. All of this activity is going on within the context of our particular 20th century Western culture. And this culture is rapidly changing from one that was very derisive about psychic matters, of which CSICOP[3] is such an excellent example, into one that accepts psychic phenomena as part and parcel of reality.

In fact in most parts of Britain the psychic world-view has always been part of the culture. When I was growing up in Scotland every big house had its white lady ghost, or its curse, from a witch 100 or more years ago.

Nowadays the public relations (PR) about witches is getting a bit better, as those excellent books by Terry Pratchett[4] and the recent Harry Potter[5] phenomenon, exemplify. However, PR aside, our cultural folk lore considers that there were people living a particular lifestyle in the remoter country areas of Britain in which psychic abilities were an integral part. Witches, like faeries, are renowned for their psychic abilities, their familiarity with magic, their ability to do the most outrageous acts, and all because they understand the psychology of the psychic and have a world-view in which the psychic is perfectly appropriate to use when needed.

One of the crafts the faeries taught to the witches was that of healing. The faery folk were renowned for their skill in healing wounds and diseases, for their knowledge of herbs. At times they communicated this knowledge to mortals, and it became one of the hallmarks of a wise woman, or a cunning man. This is classic shamanism.

There has been a huge amount of research into psychic healing by parapsychologists, which has shown that if you think about someone that this is registered by the person's body. Between 1974 and 1989, Braud and Schlitz[6] devised and ran a phenomenal series of experiments on what they call DMILS, which stands for distant mental influence on living systems. This extensive research found an EDA (talked about in chapter 1) response in a receiver when the agent in another room was either thinking for the receiver to relax, or for the receiver to become active. Obviously these different periods occurred at random so that beforehand nobody knew exactly when the sender would be trying to activate or relax the receiver. There were a total of 323 sessions, run by four different experimenters, with 62 influencers and 271 subjects. The success rate was 57%, when you would expect 50% by chance which ends up with the most enormous odds of $p < 0.000023$, which means odds of $230.000:1$.[7]

By 1991, this had been verified by others making a total of 37 experiments with 655 sessions, with 449 people (or animals) acting as receivers, 153 people as influencers, and 13 principal experimenters: $p < 10–11$, which means odds of nearly a million, million to one. During 1992 until 1996, Schlitz and Braud asked the agents just to stare at the receiver through a remote monitor, rather than trying to influence them. They performed a total of 9 studies with highly significant results; $p < 3.8 \times 10^{-6}$.[8] There are traditions and folklore across the world about the power of the gaze and its negative influence in the evil eye, as mentioned in chapter 2. This research shows quite clearly the power of the gaze.

What this says most eloquently is that if you think about someone, you affect their body; that if you merely stare at someone, even through the television, that you affect their body. Think for a moment about those times when you have been really angry. Feel the power of that emotion and the thoughts that accompany it, and realise that you are literally affecting the other person with those thoughts and feelings – in a harmful way. This is the power of hexing. Similarly, if you think of someone with love and blessings, the power of prayer, so you are affecting them for good. There has been a long term study at a cardiac hospital of patients who were being prayed for, which found that in those patients there was some significant easing of their problems. There have been hundreds of experiments looking at psychic healing, with overwhelming significant results.

Another traditional aspect of healing which has been researched recently is the blessing of the crops. We have been working with a healer on an organic farm, 'enhancing' some of the lettuce seed. The research is still quite new, but for two years there has been significantly less fungal disease in the plants grown from the enhanced seed, and the second year also found significantly enhanced yields and less slug damage.[9] Blessing the crops used to happen on Rogation Sunday, and this research suggests that there was a very good reason for doing this.

Glamourie

Glamour and illusion is central to faery magic. There are tale after tale telling how one can get totally lost through the faery art of illusion. Also tales of being given or finding faery gold and in the morning discovering only a pile of dead leaves. In one of the tales of Gwynn ap Nudd a Christian monk is invited by him to the faery halls for a banquet. After the third invitation the monk goes up to the top of the Tor and enters the castle, is greeted by Gwynn but refuses the invitation and throws holy water over everything, which promptly disappears leaving the monk on top of the cold, bare, windy Tor.

The resurgence of Eastern philosophy and techniques in the West over the past 100 years has been huge, and hundreds of thousands are now benefiting from yoga, meditation, tai chi and all the other arts and disciplines. One ideal which they hold in common with the faery faith is to pursue the spiritual path of self-knowledge and self-development first and foremost, the glamorous psychic arts (or siddhis) being considered a red-herring or sideline which you gain almost automatically when you reach a certain level, and are not to be pursued as an end in themselves. I urge all those who are interested in the development and use of psi to take note of this.

There are so many cults and people are so lost that an awful lot of damage can be done by people who are ignorant or unscrupulous. If a leader's heart is 'in the right place' and they are ignorant there will be only minimal damage, but if someone has set themselves up as a leader just for ego reasons of glamour, power and glory, then their followers can be severely hurt, as in the Jonestown massacre, or some of the followers of people who set themselves up with titles such as King of the Witches – what a ridiculous title. I personally know of one casualty of such glamourising and fooling around with young people in those heady days, and I have heard that his case is not unique. Glamour is something of which we have to be incredibly careful, which is why I stress the self-development aspect. We all know what glamorous means; we all know the effect that a glamorous person has on people; how much power over them they gain merely from the outward show. We all know the glamour and the glitter of the stage and the circus; this is one aspect of faery magic of which we must be very wary, for our egos are only too ready to trap us; humility is an essential – as long as it isn't false humility! A glamorous person is literally 'fascinating', 'entrancing.' It is really interesting to see how we use our language. What does fascinate and entrance mean?

It literally means to put another person into a trance. And we all know the power of a hypnotist over another person. I have seen a stage hypnotist entrance a dozen people – or more – out of an audience of about 150 people, probably an average of 1 in 10 people. In parapsychology we have found that a hypnotised person is highly psychic. With hypnotists who know when each person is or is not hypnotised, and with people who know their hypnotist wants them be psychic when hypnotised, psychic performance is better in the hypnotic than in the control condition. This shows the phenomenal power of suggestion, and the deep need to please that so many of us have. A person's susceptibility to hypnosis can be measured and it has been found that about 10% of people are so susceptible that they respond to a stage magician, whilst another 10% cannot be hypnotised at all, and most people are on the continuum somewhere in between. A total of 61 hypnosis–waking experiments have been run since the 1940s, and 32 had significantly better psi awareness when the person was hypnotised.[10]

The Ritual Dimension: the Cycles and the Festivals

What I want to do here is look at one aspect of the world-view linked with the fair folk, which is having a huge resurgence today, and this is the solar and lunar calendar and the corresponding festivals.

Another aspect of the lore that links the faery folk with an earlier race of people, is the connection between the fair folk and agriculture. Faery lore, and the pagan religion that is associated with it, is primarily a religion of the earth. We are heirs to a marvellously intricate system of agriculture, but developing that system took millennia, and in the early days it was vital to hold the information as clearly as possible, in a way we don't understand today because we no longer live a sustainable agriculture system. But just imagine what it would be like to have to grow all your own food, and survive all winter off it.

The faeries traditionally owned all the common and wild land until it was 'cleft by spade.' Is this another instance of antipathy to iron? Or Mother Nature being disturbed? It is regarded as a distinct breach of elfin law or privilege to till faery soil, or to remove stone, timber, or leaf from its precincts, i.e. from places we now call sacred space. If you cut a thorn tree growing on a spot sacred to the faeries, or if you violate a faery preserve of any sort, such as a faery path, or by accident interfere with a faery procession, illness and possibly death will occur. This is a link with Neolithic sacred sites, a method of preserving them from destruction. If we had kept this taboo until now, perhaps we would not be so bereft of trees or wild and open spaces – bring back the taboo! However, the lore also says that they will help on tilled land turning the soil until ready for planting – often with a bargain built in to the deed so that they receive part of the ensuing crop. In general, they were thought of as exercising control over the crops. In Savoy they are said to have taught the people the art of agriculture. Brownies and other earth sprites are guardians of the farming peasant, and assist them to grow food successfully. In the Western Isles of Scotland the top grain of corn on every stalk belonged to the good people. In that region if a person had the 'ceaird chomuinn', the association craft – a species of handicraft fellowship with the fay – he could compel them to come to his assistance for planting or reaping whenever he chose. The Tuatha of Ireland were also concerned with agriculture and the institution of festivals and ceremonies connected with it.

Thus the culture shifted from the hunter–gatherer way of life to self-sustainable agriculture – an essential part in the evolution of humanity that occurred in the Neolithic times. Agriculture became imbued with knowledge that was passed on through the ages and gradually became ritualised and mythologised. The change in season, which marks various important agricultural points in the year, came to be associated with a festival. The holy days would be marked by religious processions, dancing and feasting. Circle dancing and processional dancing were especially important and relics of these are to be found in Morris Dancing, folk or country dancing, especially those with their hobby-horses or jesters, such as at Padstow in Cornwall. The fair folk are most especially renowned for their music and dancing – circle dancing particularly in grassy places, and amongst the stone circles.

The festivals are a time when the people celebrated the turning of the wheel of the year, the life force and fertility of the land and of this beautiful planet. There is a strong emphasis in animistic religions on tuning in to the cycles of the earth, being in harmony with what is happening around us. It is a philosophy in which all of matter is infused with spirit, there is no separation between the material and the spiritual, so what we do and our attitudes affects the land and all on it. People who live a psychic lifestyle, are very concerned with the cycles and seasons; cycles of the moon, seasons of the Earth which are sun related, and the movement of the planets. The festivals mark certain moments such as dark of the moon, or full moon.

Last century at Coligny[11] in Brittany a bronze tablet was found which laid out the Celtic lunar calendar from about the 5th century. From this one can work out the lunar dates for the cross-quarter festivals. These are supposedly festivals which have been celebrated by people in Britain since whenever – no one knows. The lunar calendar is the oldest, the first, probably going back to Palaeolithic times, because the moon clearly changes from one day to the next and so is the most obvious marker of the changing days. The Moslem calendar is a purely lunar one, and the sacred month of Ramadan cycles around the year, because the moon does not correlate with the movement of the sun. Ramadan starts at dark of the moon. What some people call new moon, I call dark of the moon because for me first crescent is new moon. Dark of the moon is the time when the moon and the sun are in precisely the same position in the sky. Two days later you will see the crescent moon in the evening sky just after sunset. Two weeks later you have full moon when the moon rises as the sun sets. In the Hindu calendar, their lunar month starts just after full moon with what they call the dark fortnight, because after full moon the early part of the night is dark as the moon is rising an hour later every night, until the old crescent moon is rising just at dawn before the sun rises, and so back to dark moon. Most people reckon a lunar month to be 30 days but in fact the moon is inconstant and the month is 29.5 days, so you sometimes have a month of 30 and sometimes of 29 days. And there are $12\frac{1}{2}$ moons in each solar year. The moon does not fit into a regular number system, so to get a lunar calendar fitting in with a solar calendar lots of minor adjustments have to be made each year. The Coligny calendar shows these adjustments. I have been working with it since 1989, and have found that it runs on an identical cycle to the Chinese perpetual calendar. This means it is fine tuned to run without losing track of the solar seasonal year for at least 3000 years!!!

An interesting tale, which recurs again and again, concerns the hunchback whose hump was removed by fair folk because he reminded them of the name of a day in the week, which they had missed when chanting a rhyme on the week names. I find this a fascinating snippet of lore. It suggests to me that the fair folk held a different calendar to the Iron Age Celts. To bring in days of the week means separating the calendar from the moon, so that regular work can take place, people can receive wages, etc.

If we look at the stone circles and other megaliths we see that they are oriented primarily to the solstices and equinoxes, as well as having lunar aspects. The major solar festivals are the solstices and equinoxes, which relate to the movement of the sun. In the northern hemisphere, winter solstice is when the sun is at its most southerly point and the days are at their shortest, summer. Solstice occurs when the sun is at its most northern and the days are longest, the equinoxes being when the whole earth has equal hours light and dark.

There are folk customs all over Britain relating to these festivals. If you get a diary of British folk customs[12] you will find that some places still have festivities on the traditional date, the 21st of March, June, September and December for the equinoxes and solstices. There is an interesting historical calendrical anomaly, in which 11 days were cut out of the old Julian calendar to make the Gregorian calendar we use today, which keeps our dates more closely in line with the cycles of the sun. This means we tend to have two versions of the old festivals, since historically some people still celebrated on the old Julian calendar day, e.g. Winter solstice celebration is now Hogmanay or New Year's Eve, which is 11 days after the actual solstice day, or Michaelmas which is 11 days after the autumn equinox, or April Fools' day which is 11 days after the spring equinox.

The autumn equinox is celebrated by me at sunset, because it is the solar sunset time of year, by which I mean that from now on there will be more dark than light and with the nights drawing in it will start to get cold. I celebrate the harvest of the year. Is it a good one? What have we reaped? Are we getting ready for the dark times which begin at the Celtic festival of Samhain (Hallowe'en)? This is the mid-point of Autumn which began at Lammas (August 1st), the fullness of the harvest; and lots of churches and schools have harvest festivals at this time (Michaelmas). There are also traditionally lots of cattle fairs at this time, which nowadays are marked by the funfair arriving, because in a traditional agriculture this was the time when any surplus animals needed to be sold and slaughtered, as the people only kept those animals they could feed over the winter, those animals they would breed from in the next season.

Midsummer solstice is a huge festival in the northern hemisphere being when the days are longest and the turning point to the nights beginning to draw in again. In Britain there is a tradition that the Druids have always watched the sun rising over the Hele stone at Stonehenge and nowadays huge numbers of people go there to have a

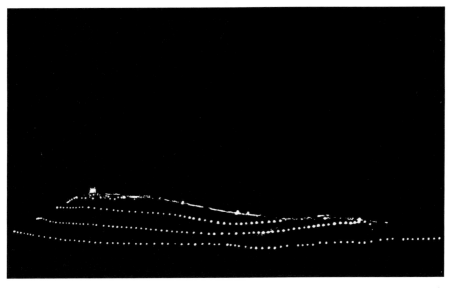

Celebrating the Millenium: in a powerful modern ritual Glastonbury Tor was lit up with 700 torch flares, each sponsored by a different person who wrote their prayer or wish for the new millenium on a card, which was attached to the flare. (Photograph courtesy of Kevin Redpath.)

festival and celebrate the shortest night and longest day. It has been subject to a huge controversy, policing, banning of the festival, but is something that cannot be stopped because people feel so intensely that this holy ceremony must be observed.

And of course midwinter solstice is our biggest festival celebrated in the West nowadays, being Christmas, and then New Year's Eve.

The spring equinox is still observed in the Christian festival of Easter (the goddess Oestre) as in 'oestrus', celebrating fertility, eggs, spring time. Easter is actually a lunar festival, related to the full moon, and the Venerable Bede[13] recounts how in 780 AD there was a controversy in Britain whether or not to use the Roman or the Celtic system for Easter. The Celtic system celebrated on the first Sunday after the full moon closest to the equinox, and so could, in some years, be before the equinox, whereas the Roman system celebrated on the first Sunday after the full moon after the equinox, and so can sometimes be almost a month after the equinox. This is the system which was adopted and is still used. What it illustrates is the Celtic lunar system of celebrating either side of the solar point, and we see this happening with the lunar cross-quarter day festivals.

Central to the Celtic calendar are the Cross-quarter days, which are half way between the solstices and the equinoxes. The year starts at

Samhain (October 31st, still celebrated as Hallowe'en), this being the time when we enter the dark of the year, not in terms of the sun which happened six weeks earlier at autumn equinox, but in terms of the season, for this is when autumn starts to turn in to winter, when the leaves on the trees are falling, when all the nuts have been gathered, after which time the blackberries are not good to eat, when frosts start to occur. Samhain is the beginning of winter, winter solstice is the fullness of winter. This is the end of the old year and the beginning of the new because, in the Celtic world-view, the dark underpins the light, and so the time of darkness comes first, as it also does in the Hindu system interestingly enough. In the Celtic Lunar calendar the day starts at sunset, for the same reason, dark coming before the light. This is why so many of our festivals are on the eve, e.g. Christmas Eve, New Year's Eve, Hallowe'en. The month starts as the moon goes in to her last quarter for this is the dark half of the moon.

In order to have the day, the moon and the season all in harmony, Samhain is celebrated when the moon enters her last quarter, which can be up to two weeks either side of October 31st. And a fire is lit to mark the moment at sunset when the day is going into the dark. We still have this celebration as Bonfire, or Guy Fawkes, Night when all over Britain bonfires are lit at sunset. Its quite a moment and really feels the full essence of going into the dark.

Imbolc is the next cross quarter day celebrated on St. Brigid's day, February 1st. (The people's celebration, left over from the calendar change, is St. Valentine's Day, the day when young would-be lovers give each other cards anonymously!) This marks the turning into spring. Although it is still winter the promise of spring is in the air. Imbolc is the turning point when one is at ultimate darkness and from now on everything will start to get less dark, the days starting to get warmer and noticeably longer day by day, the sun rising higher in the sky. Snowdrops and crocuses appear and so on. At lunar Imbolc the fire is lit at midnight when the moon is completely dark, and two to three days after lunar Imbolc is when the first crescent will appear. It feels really powerful to be celebrating at midnight at dark of the moon at this point of the year when it really is the darkest time, in an emotional and often a financial sense. This is the time when Christians celebrate Lent, a time of fasting, and in a sustainable agriculture system, one would be fasting now as the stored harvest started to run out, and there were no eggs because the hens had stopped laying, the new green vegetables had not yet started growing, etc. It is the time of year when many people suffer from depression, and so to celebrate the promise of spring to come really helps. Imbolc is when the ewes start lambing and there is milk again, and the regeneration of nature is just beginning, with spring equinox being the fullness of spring with the eggs being laid again, lots of dandelions, sorrel, burdock for salad, the time for planting potatoes and onions, etc.

The next cross-quarter day is traditionally celebrated as May Day. Celebrating lunar Beltain the fire is lit at dawn when the moon enters her first quarter marking the shift into the time of light, the turning into summer, when the seeds have been planted and everything is growing well, when the first hay harvest will soon happen, when we have light evenings again, and the movement of the sun starts to slow down after the 'rush' at spring equinox. The final cross-quarter date is Lammas, or Lughnasad when the moon is full and the fire is lit at midday, the moment of the fullness of the light, of the beginning of harvest, when the hedgerows start to bear fruit and the nuts start to ripen. Lammas is now Christianized as the Assumption of BVM – another 10-day season of an ancient Celtic Festival, similar to the twelve days of Christmas, called Yuletide, celebrating the winter solstice. Autumn equinox is the fullness of autumn, with the harvest festival, Lammas is the turning point. The cycle turns so that from now on it is going to be less light, the growing time is over and the reaping time is here and the berries are collected for wine and jam, and death makes its first approach.

Celebrating these festivals gives a real rhythm to life. Over the past twenty years I have got to know all the phases of the moon and all the phases of day and night and tune into the seasons in a way I have never tuned into them before. I watch the animals and the plants. Snowdrops are light-related in their growth: however hot or cold the winter they always flower around Imbolc. Daffodils seem to be heat-related and in a warm winter they will flower around the same time as the snowdrops, but with a cold winter they don't flower until nearer the equinox. The hawthorn always blossoms around the time of Beltain whatever the temperature, but the Elder flowers in May when winter and spring have been warm, and at summer solstice when they are cold.

For me there is a real magic in getting up in the dark and leaving the house before cockcrow to bicycle or walk to Chalice Hill and sit in the dark watching and waiting for the first tinge of less dark in the sky that tells that dawn is about to come. Learning which birds first start to sing – the cock comes first, crows are about the last – you can hear a specific sequence of their waking and giving voice, the music of the dawn, each part of the orchestra coming in in its own time. This magic is of the moment of the beauty of nature. There is no hierarchical structure, no set pattern or form I have to follow; I am following my inner spirit.

The cross-quarter days are important agriculturally rather than being turning points in the solar year, and I find it very interesting that, in the Celtic calendar, these were the important festivals. In Scotland and Ireland, right up until the middle of the 1900s, the cross-quarter days were public holidays.

I hope that in this short introduction to the old festivals you can begin to get a feeling for this world-view. Perhaps in coming to know this way of seeing the world and the lifestyle that goes with it we can allow a little bit of magic into our lives also. Many of the Christian festivals such as Candlemas (Purification of the Virgin) together with St. Valentine's Day, All Souls' Day (Hallowe'en), Christmas, May Day, Easter, are relics of former pagan festivals. This process has also opened the gates of Christian sainthood to many aspects of the Great Mother of whom St. Bridget is a classic example. By tuning in to the cycle so we help the cycle to be its fullest. This is because psychologically becoming aware of the meaning of the festivals and of the seasonal cycles that they represent we start to live a lifestyle which is in harmony with the physical body energy of the time. In winter we physically need to hibernate, to sleep lots and to move very slowly and not venture far outside. In summer we are very active and can do lots of outdoor physical work.

This principle is shown clearly by the Native Americans who live at Taos Pueblo in New Mexico. Every morning they dance in the dawn to ensure that the sun will rise. They have done this for thousands of years and the sun has always risen. According to their animistic magical principles if they stop dancing the sun will not rise. The actual fact is that they are the longest lasting pueblo in America, and if they stopped their ritual the last vestiges of their way of life, their magic, their beliefs would probably start to disintegrate as they have done for so many Indian cultures in America. So it is very important for them to keep dancing the sun up – not for the rising of the physical sun but for the maintenance of the world-view and lifestyle that they represent, and ultimately the life of this planet, which we non-spiritual Westerners have destroyed so wantonly. This is central to the synchronistic philosophy – on the one hand nature works both inwardly and outwardly to further the realisation of one's personal development. On the other hand we, through actions consistent with our highest consciousness, actions in harmony with our highest being, return to nature something that is of genuine importance to the progressive unfoldment of the whole. That is why modern society is such a tragedy, and why healing, prayer circles, spells, etc., are so efficacious. For all these things to be efficacious one must be in the Tao (in harmony with nature) when one prays, heals, works spells, etc. We all want to experience our lives as cosmologically meaningful and this world-view provides just that. Most spiritual philosophies only look to the growth of the inner self, one's personal spiritual realization. In the synchronistic way, however, nature as a whole becomes the sacred retort of the work.

This is what I feel the faery faith today to be – a resurgence in animism, a love of the earth, of nature, aware of spirit immanent in all matter, aware that my body is the temple of my soul, that I am spirit made manifest, that everything I do reverberates throughout the whole universe, that I am a part of the whole and contain the whole within me. This informs a whole way of being, a lifestyle that allows my spirituality to be part and parcel of everyday life. It is not a return to an old paganism that worships idols; it is a consciousness of our time in which the left brain analytical, abstracting ability still has its place together with the right brain mythic archetypal, and the deities are understood in their abstract mythical form, as being forces that we deal with in our growth.

The Mysteries

It is now recognised that most of the mysteries of antiquity, such as those of Eleusis, were psychic or mystical in their nature, having to do with the initiate's entrance into the underworld, or the invisible world, while out of the physical body, or else with direct communication with gods, spirits, and shades of the dead, while in the physical body. All these mysteries were performed in darkened chambers from which all light was excluded, the person often staying in such chambers for days.

This is interesting in connection with the pineal. Some research[14] has found that if you live in a room without any windows, clocks, radio, television, or anything that will give you a sense of time that, after about a week, your body will settle down to a rhythm, but it is not the normal 24 hour rhythm which is based on the sun, rather it is a 25 hour rhythm, which is based on the movement of the moon around the earth (to be precise a 24.85 hour rhythm – remember how inconstant the moon is!!). At present no one knows what links us into this time cycle, but the best bet is the pineal gland, as it is exquisitely sensitive to small changes in the GMF, and these fluctuate according to the rotation of the moon around the earth. The Mamas of Colombia spend their first seven years living in a cave and only coming out at night. In such a chamber your mind and body run on moon time alone. Can you imagine what this must do to the young child's psyche. One would be attuned to the psychic, to the numinous, not to the explicate, see-touch, sun and earth life.

I feel that New Grange, West Kennet, and the other major barrows were temples in which were celebrated ancient Mysteries, at the time when people were initiated and in which one connected directly with the Tuatha de Danaan (the gods and goddesses, with divinity), and with the land of the dead, the place of our ancestors. We make pilgrimages to these places once again at the times of the festivals. It used to be customary to spend a vigil of three, or even ten, nights and days without food or sleep, and during this time one of the fair folk, or spirit of the ancestor, would appear and speak with the person, or grant their prayer. This is directly comparable with what we know of the Greek initiation mysteries and temples at which one could invoke the help of divine beings through dreams.

Having spent many a night in vigil in a stone circle or a barrow, on top of Silbury Hill, in Lough Crew cairn, on top of Carn Ingli (The Hill of the Angels) whose rocks are so magnetic that they spin a compass, and more other places than I can mention here, I can most certainly appreciate that spending a three-day fast inside a tumulus would be a deeply mystical experience, especially with a mind trained to go out-of-body, or to deep meditation, or some other altered state of consciousness. Fasting in itself makes one lighter, less earth-bound, more prone to waking hallucinations and other mystical experiences. It is of interest to note here that all the initiation chambers, like New Grange, are specifically oriented towards a specific star or sun or moonrise. They are astronomically precise as well as being Faraday chambers in power spots. For example, New Grange is oriented $43° 60'$ S.E. and so is oriented to the winter solstice sunrise as is Gavrinis, another initiation chamber in Brittany, and Stony Littleton, the largest barrow with seven chambers in Somerset (although someone told me it was oriented to the major lunar standstill which is slightly different from the sun). As I mentioned in chapter 1, I have had a very strong experience in Lough Crew chambered cairn in which I felt as though I stood on the threshold of the otherworld. And that was just one night – imagine what 10 days would do.

There seems to be an added element in lying or sitting in particular stone that accentuates the mystical effect of the place. These shallow basins are found in the cells at Lough Crew, New Grange and Dowth. So, once again we have this mystic connection with stone; probably granite which is heavily crystalline stone – imagine what that would do to your electromagnetic energies, let alone at the psychological level.

The practice of pilgrimage has, of course, been continued by the Christians, and Evans Wentz[15] says that in Ireland the Christian pilgrims used to use the stone troughs or beds that are sometimes found in the barrows, like the sarcophagi found in the Pyramids. I had an amazing experience once when I was 22. I was intending to visit Ethiopia during my summer vacation. The previous year I had visited Egypt, so this year I flew in to Cairo from Athens, arriving in Cairo at dawn, and went straight to the train station to book my ticket on the train for Aswan, as I did not want to spend time in Egypt. My train left at sunset, so I had a day to spend in Cairo. I went immediately on a bus to the pyramids, arriving there so early that even the guides and their camels were asleep. With my pack on my back I crawled into the second pyramid and went down to the Queen's chamber, took off my pack and sat down. At this time I had not done any form of yoga or meditation, or any other practice, and I sat there for a while, noticing how sound from people visiting the Queen's chamber could be heard as if there was no distance, how the space felt as if there was nothing there despite the thousands of tons of stone above my head. On a couple of occasions a guide brought a group into the chamber and I smiled hello. After a while I got bored and decided to leave to get some food. When I got outside I discovered it was late in the afternoon and I only just got to the train in time. What I had thought to be an hour or two turned out to be 8 hours!!

The chambers, the stone troughs, are very similar in basic structure to certain of the Egyptian, Greek, Peruvian and Indian temples, with their chambers, stone chests, etc. The symbology of facing East to the rising sun and rising moon, to new birth, dawn life, etc., and facing West to the setting sun and setting moon, to night, death, etc., are the two parts of the whole found in every religion, and implicit in all of our spiritual beings.

Finn MacCoul's Lake, also called St. Patrick's Purgatory, was used right up to the 17th century as a place of initiation and pilgrimage;[16] then it was destroyed by the English. It was considered a place of entrance to the Underworld. The person fasted for 15 days prior to an all-night vigil in which a mystic bridge was crossed to a celestial city. If one ate food in the city one was bound forever there. These rites lasted from 1st to 15th August, the whole of Lughnasadh (Lammastide).

Evan Wentz[17] considers that at Dun Aengus, the mystic assemblies and rites, conducted in such a sun-temple, so secure and so strongly fortified against intrusion, represented a somewhat different mystical school, one very much older than at New Grange. Like others he considers that all the megalithic structures were places for practical spiritual purpose, and notes that since the ancient Celts never separated civil and religious functions, such temples could have been as frequently used for non-religious assemblies as for initiation and other ceremonies, since there is no split between secular and spiritual. For example, in the Isle of Man the sacred mound is still used for confirming the government's new laws.

Let us note this point and take it to heart. There is to be no separation of our civil and our religious life. Every breath, every thought, every word and every action is both secular and spiritual. This above all is what the science and art of magic teach.

135

The Science of Magic

The science and art of magic IS the science and art of the mind, the psyche, together with our emotions and our soul and spirit. Magic obeys psychological laws. The world of spirits, of psychic phenomena, is the world of the mind.

According to Evans Wentz, the first thing taught to a neophyte was self-control. The magical science taught that by formulas of invocation, by chants, by sounds, by music, by movement such as dancing in circles, by meditation, by fasting, by going at night at certain phases of the moon to the sacred places that these invisible beings, the fair folk, could be joined with to help at a magical level. The original magic was to work together with the elemental beings, with the devas, with the earth energies, and their link with the rest of the solar system and the universe. We no longer follow the old patriarchal attempt to control Mother Nature, rather we teach ourselves self-discipline and pit our wills to control our own unruly minds and emotions and personality problems, so that we can best live in harmony with the universe. In fact the patriarchal magic of control over spirit beings such as in tales of Victorian Golden Dawn ritualises a later patriarchal magic for the older faery faith talks about marriage, or consort with the fair folk, working with rather than control over the daemonic realm.

The essential facet is that self-control, self-discipline, is the absolute basic first step in training the mind. I have noticed this again and again with people coming to learn yoga. The very first lesson they have to learn is the self-discipline of actually coming to the class each week. The mind is a tricksy thing, about as tricksy as a piskie, and will find any and every excuse not to do that which it knows is good for it. Working with the mind is like working with a recalcitrant 3 year old. Only when you have taught your mind that you WILL do what you want, that you are in charge and not it, can you hope to get anywhere in any form of self-development, spiritual growth or training your psychic abilities, which are the tools of magic.

The particular magical tools for linking with the fay spirits are chanting, sound and music, the tools of enchantment. This is what we are beginning to learn about now. Tibetan overtone chanting, yogic OM chanting, even Gregorian chanting is being revived by thousands all over the world. And some are even chanting and dancing in the stone circles. The same with magical sounds. Have you ever sat on a moonlit night in a stone circle with the Aboriginal digeridoo playing. Magic; pure magic. Some people talk about energy being raised. I know what they mean – it's that tingle along the spine, that shiver in the body; that's magic sound in a stone circle, and more and more are experiencing such magic. And music; the playing of pipes, of a whole range of drums, and other instruments that come from the dawning of humanity's music. These evoke that same quality. None of this is high magic; it's natural magic, peasant magic, pagan magic, the magic of the earth, the magic that brings the earth alive. Simple, spontaneous, as the mood takes one, coming from inspiration and not from dogma. This is the birthing of a new spirituality, that is as yet formless, nameless and growing. This is the essence of all religion, this atunement of spirit, this growing of oneself so that one becomes more and more sensitive and more and more able to tune in to the feeling of the place and time – without losing your stability. That's another reason for self-discipline. This is why we have to work on our minds, our emotions, our personality, our being.

6

The Faery Faith Philosophy.
The Developing Spirituality
of the Aquarian Age

Theology is ultimately political. The way human communities
deify the transcendent and determine the categories of good and evil
have more to do with the power dynamics of the social systems
which create the theologies than with the spontaneous revelation of
truth from another quarter.

(Stone, 1979)[1]

Every spirituality has its mythic aspect, its ethical and moral aspect, the social and experiential aspects. The modern day conceptions of the holo-graphic universe, reincarnation, eco-green awareness in everyday life, personal self-development through psychotherapy are all aspects of a mystical philosophy being reborn in our time. The faery faith is an integral part of this revival.

The following ideas arise directly from my having lived in Glastonbury, the ancient Isle of Avalon, for the past 22 years. I feel that this magical place is fertile soil for spiritual growth, which makes it an incredibly hard place to live in because the lessons come thick and fast. But then throughout the ages people have lived at sacred sites specifically for initiation, for spiritual learning and growth – they are not places in which to live if you want an ordinary life!

Precession of the Equinoxes

Astronomically, the rising constellation of stars in the sky at the spring equinox, just as the day is dawning, is changing slowly over this century and the next from that of the sign of Pisces to that of Aquarius. One cannot put a precise date on the dawning of the Age of Aquarius because in fact the stars of these two signs overlap in the sky, so this change is very slow and intermingled, moving from one influence to the next in a subtle manner. The first of the Aquarian stars will be rising at the spring equinox sometime around 2200 CE; the last of the Piscean stars will still be rising around 3000 CE! In our latitude, dawn precedes sunrise by about an hour or so depending on time of year – translate this into precession-of-equinox terms when one day is equivalent to about 2200 years, and dawn could start at least 200 years before the first star-rise, so to speak, which is why we are celebrating the dawning of the Age of Aquarius now. Dawn is that wonderful magical time when the light gradually, imperceptibly starts to silver in the eastern sky, a time of peace when the world is just waking, the cock is crowing, the first crow flaps lazily across the sky, the first colours begin to show in the land. For the Celtic and many tribal people this time of transition is felt to be the crack in the cosmic egg when magic can occur most easily, when the veils are thinnest between the worlds. Hence, the times in which we live are certainly very interesting and there is massive change afoot.

In looking ahead to the Aquarian Age, it may be helpful to have a perspective of where we are coming from: the Age of Pisces was from approximately 0 to 2000 CE, before that the Age of Aries was from 2000 BCE to 0, and before that, from 4000 BCE to 2000 BCE, there was the Age of Taurus. The Taurean Age was the age of the change from Neolithic to Bronze Age, from Goddess as deity supreme, to one in which she reigned with her consort, as for example Inanna with Dumuzzi. The Minoan civilisation of Crete, the last of the Goddess cultures to survive, symbolises this age well with its snake priestesses and the Minotaur – the Taurean bull. As the Age of Taurus advanced so the goddess's consort became stronger, until the day came when he, as the Greek hero Theseus with Ariadne's help, was strong enough to kill the Minotaur, and the Age of Aries came into its own, the sun god hero reigning supreme, humanity's culture shifting from the Bronze into the Iron Age. At the latter end of this time (the beginning starting really as early as 600 BCE with the birth of the Buddha), the spirituality of humanity shifted away from the sun god and into monotheistic patriarchal religions such as Christianity and Islam. This spirituality is of the Piscean Age, but where are the myths celebrating the death of the ram in the same way that the death of the bull was celebrated at the turning into the Age of Aries? What has happened to our mythology here? – oh dear! we find that Christ is not only the fisher of men but also the good shepherd, the lamb carries the flag, the flag being a martial Arian symbol for sure. The ram is alive and well in the age of the fish, and so the martial energy of Aries did not die out in the past two millennia but has carried on, almost to the death of us all in the ultimate scenario of nuclear war.

A thought that occurs is that Western astrology is still linked to this time as it takes Aries as the rising sign at the spring equinox, rather than Pisces. Symbolically this means that in some way the Western world is still linked into the Arian sun god, martial ethos. Maybe it is time for a change, to shift the energy at this symbolic, mythic level.

Each age has its own spirituality. This is evolving as our consciousness evolves. And now we are shifting to the Age of Aquarius. I feel we must make certain that the lamb and the fish both are ritually slain in this shift; let us go through to the new having cast off the skin of the old thoroughly. Only in this way can we grow true and strong, leaving behind that which has served its purpose and is no longer appropriate for the new. Mythology is a central aspect of spirituality, so let us create our Aquarian myths with wisdom. For example, one thing I have noticed is that symbol of Aquarius is the water-carrier, a noticeably androgynous figure. It is essentially gender free, neither male nor female and partaking of characteristics of both, as do the angels. And we are entering a time of more equality between the sexes which will mark a huge shift in our world-view, in the way in which we actually live our lives on this planet. At this time in the West, there is far more acceptance of homosexuality, and of each of us owning our opposite gender characteristics whatever physical gender we are born. This is one of the characteristics of the fool, and so maybe the symbology of the fool has a particular teaching for us in this next age.

The Politics of Spirituality

It appears that our social system is once again shifting to permit this faery philosophy back in to our culture. Spirituality is political because it underpins every moment of our being. Essentially, when I look to the emerging spirituality dawning in our day, I see an era in which the spiritual regains its place alongside the material. Our world-view is our religion so we must constantly revise and extend our understanding.

In the coming Aquarian spirituality I see that we are at an evolution of psyche. The mother goddess was there at the dawning of humanity, during the early childhood of humanity, to nurture and love and care for us, from whom we could ask for things, or to put things right for us. The human race has evolved from the childhood of Mother worship through to the adolescence of Father worship, in which we had a father god making the laws and making sure we behaved ourselves correctly. In adolescence we need the father to encourage us to grow to our full potential, using both carrot and stick. Now we are growing up to adulthood and taking the roles of father and mother into ourselves. We are becoming both god and goddess, celebrating our divinity, and becoming self-responsible for our actions, our thoughts, our feelings, our behaviour – no longer blaming it on something outside ourselves or looking to an outside force to put it right. In this philosophy there is no god/goddess out there, who will judge us and punish us and forgive us, rather the god and the goddess are within and we are growing into our divinity, incorporating the 'Divine' within ourselves. Now we are coming into our maturity and we need to be totally self responsible.

I think that the faery faith permits a progression whereby we transcend the old religions. We are learning how to harmonise the subconscious with the conscious so as to create the supraconscious within our own selves. Some see this more in terms of the equalisation of the right with the left as seen in terms of cerebral hemispheres. In its outer form this can be seen as the harmonisation of the matriarchal and patriarchal religions, a joining of East and West, of the old and the new.

Living the Synchronistic Way

In conclusion, the essence of the faery faith is a mystical animism. Mysticism is fundamentally the same in all ages and among all peoples. Modern mysticism (derived mainly from oriental sources) has affected Celtic mysticism as handed down from the dim past, because the two occupy a common psychical territory. Ironically, with the new physics, an animistic view of man is more in harmony with scientific premises than any other. The ideas associated with faeries strike at the very roots of human belief. Animism is considered to be the oldest religion in the world; the cradle of all sects, cults, and theologies of humanity.

The Holographic Paradigm,[2] by Wilber, and *Wholeness and the Implicate Order*,[3] by Bohm, offer a world-view that is closely linked with what Huxley calls 'The Perennial Philosophy'[4] of mystics of all ages. This states that Spirit is the ground of all being, that which is immanent in all nature, as well as being our highest ideal to which we strive – we are spirit real-ising itself. It is all and everything at one and the same time. All is interlinked, all is one. This entails a society which does not work in a hierarchical pattern, but one that sees each part of the whole as an essential ingredient, no one better or more important than the other – the essence of the cooperative movement. Or, as I call it, living in circle, which is incredibly difficult to do, but part of the essential shift out of the old Piscean hierarchical way. In Glastonbury we have a community Assembly Rooms in which we have been, and we are still, struggling with this change from the old hierarchical to the new cooperative, communal way of working. When things are as deep rooted as a 2000 year old world-view, then it takes more than one generation to make the shift. We are looking long term here.

Central to this emerging holographic world-view is what I call 'living the synchronistic way' in which outer events in nature link in with one's inner psychic state. For me our spirituality is a practical process of self-development, and synchronistic happenings are an integral part of that process, letting us know that we are getting it right – or wrong as the case may be. Truly understanding the psychic brings one to the holographic world-view, and of course synchronicity is the outer event which brings this to light in a truly wonderful, exciting way. And such experiences necessarily entail us seeing the truth which our subconscious is presenting to us, because like dreams, synchronistic experiences bring out the truth of our deep level psyches.

When we become aware of the holographic nature, the total interlinking that occurs at the deeper unconscious layers, so we live with this interlinking as our central motive force. Both archetypal and synchronistic events exhibit the property that transcendental meaning can manifest itself simultaneously in our inner psyches and in the outer world. Meaning is as major a force in life as is matter and energy. A familiar example of this is the Tarot, I Ching or runic divination practices. In all of these one uses randomicity, e.g., shuffling the pack, or throwing the coins, to permit synchronicity to occur, in which the spread of the cards, or the hexagram that results, has meaning to the person in accordance with the question, the focus of intent with which they performed the divination. The essential idea is that the universe mirrors back in accordance with one's intent. The meaning that one often feels overwhelmed by in synchronistic occurrences is a transcendental meaning present in nature itself. The Collective Unconscious is a universal substrate present in the environment, an atmosphere in which we live. This is so important to me – our spirituality is that of nature herself – our deepest unconscious and the archetypes are the consciousness or spirituality of the planet itself.

Ethical Dimension: Pachamama – the Earth is our Mother

The Aquarian spirituality is a very personal spirituality because the Aquarian archetype is that of the individual within the collective.

There is no dogma laid down from outside; you choose your own path from the 'spiritual supermarket.'[5] Never before in the history of humanity have all the world's great religious teachings been available for us to pick and choose from – now they are. So each of us has our own cauldron, our own stewpot, and into it we put in those spiritual philosophies which suit us for our own growth, our own needs. This is a grass roots spirituality which seems to be coming up from the very earth: we are evolving because the planet is evolving; we are the conscious myth-making, acting-out aspect of her spiritual growth. Or is it the spiritual growth of the universe, are we the universe evolving? Perhaps we can see it as us being the microcosm of the macrocosm, the ancient teachings of 'as above, so below' applying in every way in everything we do.

This is not a selfish philosophy where one is good because at the end one is rewarded, as in the Piscean Age philosophies. It is for the good of the whole, for the evolution of the whole, that one behaves as one does. There is no ultimate end, it is all in the process. Under the emerging holographic philosophy, where the whole is present in each part, and no part can do anything without affecting the whole, we are wholly part of the Universe and it is up to each individual to change their lifestyle in accord with the planet's needs, in harmony with the planet, a lifestyle that the earth can support. As guardians and gardeners tending with love and care our own bodies and hearts and minds, which are miracles of creation, and feeling the pure pleasure of this 'temple of the soul', of our homes and each other, so we live lightly on the Earth and create beauty all around us. We need to fully 'walk our talk'.

There is great emphasis on each individual living their beliefs every day at every moment, living a spiritual awareness of the inter-connectedness of everything at every level. The realisation that all is interwoven, interlinked, must surely create a change in practical life attitudes, changes that are apparent everywhere now – after 30 years of pushing for them!

Just as I was writing this book I was interviewed by a Canadian person who was doing a postgraduate thesis on sacred space, and we talked about creating sacred space in everyday life. I had never formalized how I live before and it was quite an eye opener to me to see so clearly what I do. The first thing we noticed is that my kitchen has become a sacred space. It is not only a kitchen and living room but also the place where I do my yoga and meditation, and we found that there were four altars in the room, which I lovingly and regularly tend. What turned the mantlepiece into an altar were the figures of goddesses, of Buddha, candles and incense on it, and these get lit regularly at special moments. Even the table was an altar on which there is a candle,

143

which I buy specially at the beginning of each lunar month to represent the aspects of the coming month or season, and this candle is lit before eating supper. This means that the food is dedicated to the mother, to nature and we say thanks in a fairly relaxed way before eating, but that feeling of the sacred is there. In creating sacred space what I realised is that it is taking the everyday and giving it just a little tweak so that one is aligned with the fundamental basis of the spirit of the universe. It's the attitude with which we do things that transforms it from the secular to the sacred. Having altars in one's kitchen brings the temple into the home, and the hearth, the heart of the home, becomes sacred and is an integral part of daily life. Another example, I have a wood burning stove in the kitchen which heats the water and the radiators. The wood I burn on this stove comes from some woodland in which I have a share, and I go out and coppice the ash trees so that there is a totally sustainable resource heating my home which I tend. The feeling from burning that wood and heating my home and water with it is so wholesome, so nurturing, the hearth has become sacred.

There are faeries at the bottom of my garden underneath the hawthorn tree, a wild patch where I never dig or plant things, just leave it. One spring day I took a saucer of food out from a very special Bridie doll tea party, and when I went to collect the saucer there were seven hawthorn berries on that saucer. It felt like a thank you from the faeries. Hawthorn berries occur in autumn, this was March. The orchard beyond the hedge has a well in it, St. Edmund's Well, one of the six sacred wells of Avalon, and the farmer has never used chemicals on his land. The orchard was planted after the first world war and the old cider apples are so beautiful. He cares for this land in the old fashioned way, he is like someone out of Thomas Hardy, another century, and the land has a vitality and beauty to it that is numinous, and I can honestly say I have seen the faeries there.

All the earth is sacred and honouring that by caring for it with the attitude of sacred allows the spirit to shine, that extra feeling of vitality. Experiencing this starts by seeing the beauty of land that is cared for with so much love and care, and then allowing oneself to feel the spirit of it. This is a choice. I call it the type of eyes you use to look with. You can look with the everyday eyes and see the mist on the grass and flowers, or you can look with the other eyes, the eyes of a child, and see the devic life, the faeries playing. It's like love, you have to allow yourself to be open to it. Mostly we close ourselves off because of fear of being hurt or what-ever. Just a tweak of an attitude and it's all there.

One of the main inspirations to me at the moment is the vision of all of the Universe as the dance of spirit in manifestation as matter: the Gaia Hypothesis[6] and quantum physics combined. My inspiration comes from both sources and is a fusion of the two. Thus to me spirit and matter are two aspects of the same thing seen from different perspectives. When I wonder at the beauty of nature, of sunsets, moonrise, rainbows, mountains, the oceans, plants, insects, butterflies, animals and our bodies, I am seeing a miracle of creation awesome in its being. And this wonder is a mixture of the spiritual perception of the moment together with the scientific knowledge of the complexity of the detail and how it all works.

Our consciousness I am sure is very different now. It is only in the past 100 years that most Western people, and an ever-increasing proportion of Asian and African people, have been able to read and write; and the type of left-brain consciousness associated with literacy is a very different type of consciousness than that associated with an oral society. At present there is a big movement to bring our highly developed literary consciousness to focus in on our dream mind, our left hemisphere is joining with the right hemisphere, or perhaps our conscious is joining with our subconscious, and my feeling is that this is part of an enormous evolutionary shift in consciousness, in which analytical mind and global holistic mind work together equally. This is very exciting because it is possible that a new sort of consciousness develops from this merging (that this is the next step in the evolution of consciousness), or maybe this is the state of enlightenment, of true deep understanding. I think that the grass roots growth of the new spirituality is linked to this consciousness shift that is occurring, the results of which are yet to be realised.

Of course, the new that is growing today is actually a very old spirituality indeed, in that it is the shamanic magical world-view. What makes me call it 'new' is that I doubt whether Neolithic people used the highly intellectual abstract constructs we use today.

Experiential Dimension: Personal Growth – Watching out for Ego and Developing the Divine Within

Spiritual growth, evolution of consciousness, is the continuous work of bringing our conscious self-concept into progressively greater accord with reality. When we become spiritually realised we become enlightened, which I am beginning to see means total understanding, total clarity, awareness, no more confusion, a head working with the heart so that our emotions, and physical feelings, and needs are dealt with appropriately. Imagine always knowing what is the best thing to do feel, say or think, knowing the perfect way to be!

Love is the very act of evolution, of self-development, of spiritual growth, the way in which we grow towards divinity. It is constant work – we have to work at loving, being courageous and facing our fears. It is very painful indeed; the spiritual path is difficult, we have to work to understand. Each one of us, in our daily struggle to become a more aware loving person, is an integral part of the spiritual growth and development of the Universe; in our daily attempts to become enlightened we are divinity growing. In the holographic philosophy where the whole is present in every part, so we can see that divinity is present in everything. There is no divine separate from us out there. We are god and goddess and spirit in evolution. With this philosophy, every action is done with regard to the essential spirit of everything, with love, with passion, rejoicing in emotion, in feeling, alive in every sense.

This means we accept our shadow side within as well, instead of forever projecting it out onto other people and their spiritual concepts, scapegoating other religions etc., but recognising that what we hate most outside of us is an aspect of that which we find most difficult to deal with within ourselves. All polarity splits, conscious/unconscious, subject/object, male/female, dark/light, black/white, positive/negative, etc., become healed in the knowing of the unitary nature of the universe. We are beginning to accept the nasty, the bad, the evil, the ignorant as an integral part of the whole. When we invoke one the other, its flip side is also invoked.

For me this whole psychological aspect of our spirituality is one of the central aspects of what I am conceiving as the new spirituality: witness the enormous growth of depth, humanistic and transpersonal psychology over the past twenty years. The psychotherapy movement, which has made such a change in our way of thinking over the past five decades, is an essential aspect of the new spirituality in that it helps us to overcome our personal problems, to delve down into the roots of why we are so dysfunctional and make such serious mistakes in our lives, creating such troubles as alcoholism, drug dependency, abuse of women, children, employees and outsiders, wars, avarice – the dreadful greed which is threatening life on this planet.

The energy engendered by emotion is probably the strongest energy of our body/minds, with the emotional energy engendered by religious beliefs possibly the most destructive, as seen in the various religious wars around the world. We are dealing here with issues that encompass more than the rational – more than reason or the purely intellectual. There is always an emotional component, however much it may be dressed up in logical rationalism. The results of this locking up of our spiritual awareness and the spiritual aspect of life has led directly to the material problems confronting our generation.

The negative spiritual aspect of the mind has often been conceptualised as demonic, and we disregard demons at our peril for they are reappearing as mass psychoses in our prisons and mental hospitals, which are overflowing with violent, aggressive, crazy people. And the demons are also around us in our ever-increasing materialistic life-style which is destroying the sacred

Social and Ritual Dimension: the Cycles

The whole supports the individual and in its turn the whole requires the support of each individual. Each person must act as a type of facilitator of the unfoldment of the events in nature itself, growing within the whole that is unfolding. This is a typically Aquarian statement! The new that is emerging is Earth-centred and so we tune in to the cycles and seasons, cycles of the moon, seasons of the Earth which are sun related, and to the planets. And so there is a place for marking certain moments, the festival times. That which we do ritually enables the symbolic idea to then manifest practically in our everyday lives.

One thing that amuses me is that at present we can celebrate every festival at least three or four times: for instance on the traditional date, say June 21st, March, etc., for the equinoxes and solstices; or you can take the precise astrological moment when the sun moves into the appropriate sign, or according to the moon, say Easter at spring equinox, full moon and so on. It's really great fun because you can spend about 10 days celebrating each festival and as they come around at least every six weeks, that's a lot of time spent celebrating!

I have yet to see the same thing happening twice on any of these festival days. We are finding out new ways of honouring these times, and at present it is pretty chaotic, spontaneous; there is no structure, no set pattern or form to follow; we can follow our inner spirit. Perhaps there is some need sometimes for a certain amount of structure, of for-malised ritual, but I don't think we have found the right structures yet. People cast circles, invoke deities and guardians, use incense, candles and crystals, and these are all excellent tools to help create a suitable atmosphere. That is all. They are an excellent psychological ploy to help the mind shift into that special space in which the mystery is tangible. If we recognise this perhaps we can allow more flexibility in, let our intuition seize the moment so that we don't have the deadness that can be present at dogmatised rituals. Structuring and formalising is not part of the Aquarian spirit which is much more airy and watery, free flowing. Structuring, creating dogma is of the old mode concerned with power over, control over. We are having to go through our fear that without formality there will be nothing. We are having to learn to flow with the moment, with knowing when there is a need to hold energy, when there is a need to let it go.

Central to this is opening up to and being aware of the unconscious, working with our dreams, with creative imagination and visualisation. There are techniques which can be done to help one shift into a state of consciousness in which one is more likely to have a profound mystical experience, such as yoga, meditation, using certain plants, fasting, lack of sleep, chanting, drumming, dancing, being in certain places at certain times, such as being at a sacred site all night of the full moon, and these are becoming more and more practised and popular. And then the actual mystical, magical experience can happen at any time (particularly when you least expect it!), and that is the life-blood of this spirituality.

Let me give a small example of this personal individual belief within the collective with the new age version of the chakra system. The notion of chakras comes from the Hindu religion, from which the West has received yoga, the idea of karma and many other spiritual ideas over the past 100 years.

The new age view of the chakras is not the Hindu version. It is a new creation that people in the West have developed. For instance, people think of the chakras as having colours of the rainbow with the bottom chakra being red, then orange, then yellow through to indigo at the eyebrow centre and violet at the crown. The Hindu system is very different because each chakra has colours of the lotus petals and then colours of the design within the lotus. So for instance mooladhara the root lotus has red petals with a yellow square yantra inside; swadhistana has a vermilion lotus with a silver or white crescent moon inside; manipura has a dark blue lotus with a red triangle yantra; anahata has a vermilion lotus with a smoky six-pointed star yantra; vishuddhi has a pure blue lotus with a violet circle yantra and ajna has a clear or grey lotus with a clear or grey circle.

Another example of the difference is in the location. The modern Western system has the root chakra at the same place as the Hindu located in the perineum for men and the cervix for women, but then the Hindu system has swadisthana at the sacrum and the Western places it farther up the body, just below the navel. The Hindu has manipura at the navel and the Western places it farther up the body at the solar plexus, just below the diaphragm. The Hindu has anahata at the heart which is between the breasts, the Western system places it higher up on the chest. Now I am not sure about this. Perhaps we have a new spiritual system developing, which has its own inbuilt validity. Or is it something that will die out as the new age dies out once Aquarian spirituality no longer becomes new. The yogis say that their system is 4000 years old and so will remain because it is solid. All I know is that people are best to be informed of the differences so that they can make their choice,

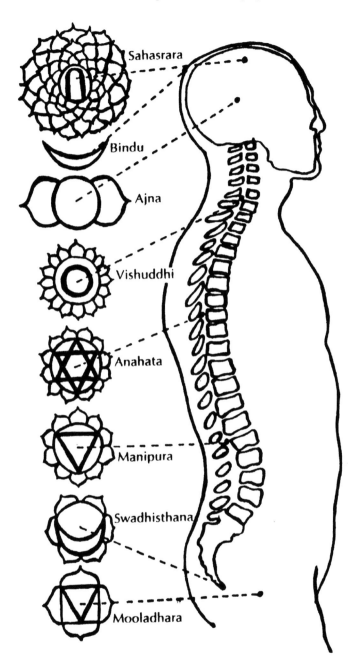

The traditional Hindu location of the Chakras and their associated yantras (Illustration courtesy of Bihar School of Yoga. Reproduced from A Systematic Course in the Ancient Tantric Techniques of Yoga and Kriya *by Swami Satyananda Saraswati, Bihar School of Yoga, 1989, p. 488)*

149

rather than accepting the new Western system as the correct system out of ignorance of the original Hindu version.

Faery Science: the Quantum Self

Parapsychology is the scientific investigation of our psychic abilities and the psychology of those states of mind most conducive to the practice of the psychic gifts for healing, clairvoyance, divination, etc. In doing such research, parapsychology seems to be uncovering the basic root elements of all religions, the perennial philosophy.

Through psi we are potentially omniscient and omnipotent, i.e. divine. The one thing unclear from this see–touch reality of ours is how psi works. Through parapsychology we are understanding what happens once the information is in the brain so to speak, the psychology of psi, but how does it get there in the first place. For this we have to look at the quantum world-view that is emerging from modern physics.

In altered states our brains change. There are billions of connections between the neurons; during waking consciousness there are about one million at what is called quantum threshold of sensitivity; during sleep, hypnosis, etc., there are about one thousand million at quantum threshold, i.e. a quantum event can trigger the synapse; our mind linked with our brain; thus in altered states we are more susceptible to this quantum reality. There is a part of us working, living in the strange Alice in Wonderland reality of quantum physics.

Karl Pribram[7], in his work on memory, considers that the brain works by building up neural nets that utilise the holographic principle of information storage. Our minds work in this way. Each part contains information about the whole. The form and structure of the entire body–mind may be said to be enfolded within each region of the brain. It is at the synapses that the processing of the incoming sensory information is accomplished. Not only memory and sensory experiences have been incorporated into this holographic model of the brain but also imaging and visualisation. These are part of the psi process. This holographic principle is characteristic not only of brain processing but of physical reality as well. What is organism is no longer sharply distinguished from what lies outside the boundaries of the skin. 'In the holographic domain each organism represents in some manner the universe and each portion of the universe represents in some manner the organisms within it.'[8]

'There are intriguing implications in a paradigm that says the brain employs a holographic process to abstract from a holographic domain.'[9] One needs no energy of transmission for psi since this information emerges from a reality transcending time and space – we are linked to everything that ever was, is or will be. Psychic phenomena are by-products of the simultaneous-everywhere matrix. Individual brains are bits of the greater hologram; they have access under certain circumstances to all the information in the total system. In *The Holographic Paradox*, Stanley Krippner[10] states that this theory means that paranormal phenomena would have to be postulated as part of the theory, had there not been documented occurrences throughout human history. Thus all psychic phenomena lose much of their bizarre quality and find their place within a philosophy of the Universe.

Since the work of the great physicists such as Schrödinger, Heisenberg and Einstein, we have a new world-view in which energy equals matter times the speed of light squared! Matter and energy are two sides of same coin; we can look at one side or at the other, but cannot completely know both at once. Reality at its most primary level consists not of fixed actualities that we can know but rather of all the probabilities that we might know. An electron can manifest as a particle or as an energy wave; the same applies to a photon. Anything can happen. This is a probabilistic universe in which the individual can never be wholly known of itself; hence free will and fate. Fate is the probability of the whole, but the individual is totally random. You and I are probabilities with infinite possibility for change. In choosing whether to manifest particle or wave, matter or energy, so we define the reality in which we wish to live – that of matter or that of energy, which in human terms can be conceived to be some form of spirit.

It seems as if it is will and consciousness that define this world. Eddington and others see the world more as a great mind than as a great machine – mind is the primary reality, psychological laws are primary and physical matter laws only secondary. In the mind time and space are irrelevant, hence psi and the holographic universe. When any physical process starts it sends out feelers in all directions, feelers in which time and space may be reversed; in which normal rules are violated and anything may happen. This is called the virtual state – if you can't decide whether to stay at home or go to the seaside you'll be mentally in both places at once – a most uncomfortable position until you have 'made up your mind' and collapse your wave function into one reality.

Our physical world is not a structure built out of independent entities but rather a web of relationships between elements whose meanings arise wholly from their relationships to the whole. ALL living beings are projections of a single totality so my thoughts are connected with those of others; all are intimately interconnected, which leads us back to psi.

The implications of Bohm's ideas are that the easily accessible contents of consciousness are included within a much greater implicit

151

background the personal subconscious, which is contained within a much greater background the unconscious, which is contained within the world mind or collective unconscious. Telepathy, clairvoyance, precognition and the various forms of mind over matter arise from this conception of consciousness as the explicit modes of action and perception of this implicate higher dimensional ground of being. That is why they have no known forms of energy transmission, because they arise from a realm that is everywhere at all times. So the primary reality is mental.

Psychotropic Plants

Of course, the traditional shamanic practice for entering an altered state for magical purposes has always been to use those magical plants that Nature has supplied so liberally. In Britain nowadays people use magic mushrooms, *Psilocybin*, which as far as I am concerned give direct access to the faery realms. They are sometimes called pixie caps because that is what they look like and I have been in the faery court having eaten a few of these. We also have the fly agaric, traditional Tunguska shaman mushrooms in Britain, but they are far stronger and I wouldn't advise anyone to use them unless they are with someone who is skilled in their use. For the problem with our present day culture is that we have no respect. These sacred plants, which take us into faery or other spirit realms, are not really meant to be recreational drugs – just as tobacco is a sacred herb to be used in ritual on special occasions, for it is a very powerful drug. But us Westerners misuse so casually. When we can learn to respect the power of what nature provides and use it in full ceremony, then we have the transformative, mystical experience that is the full potential of these plants. Which is not to say that taking them casually has no effect – of course it has very strong effects which can be very beneficial, but the risks are higher because you may have a bad trip, and that can lead to mental hospital, nervous breakdown, blowing several fuses and either taking years to recover or not recovering at all. Having said this, a psychedelic experience profoundly moves the person, and it is this which is of such value. Once experienced, never forgotten. The world is never the same again, and this can be a necessary spur to undertaking the arduous training and self-discipline which is the real goal.

I know that whilst taking the various psychotropics was an important part of my growth and development, even more important has been the decades of practising a spiritual discipline, in my case yoga and meditation. How I understand it, is that the plants are like a jet plane and give us a boost which allows to enter the other realms

Amanita muscaria

Fly agaric mushrooms; these are the gifts from Nature which enable Santa Claus to fly every Christmas Eve (Illustration reproduced from A guide to British Psilocybin Mushrooms *by Richard Cooper, Hassle Free Press, 1977.*

through their power. The real work comes when we return to earth, and then we have to learn how to go there using our own power. And doing this develops strength of character, discipline, love, beauty of being, fullness of heart, and all those other worthwhile qualities that turn us into people who we would like to know, who do more good than harm in this world. This is really hard work and it takes a lifetime.

Animism has survived through millennia because its philosophy is fluid, because it is able to adapt itself to changing conditions, and is relevant to life whatever the context, because it is primarily a Nature religion. Thus as we eve-olve, as does all of Nature, so Darwin and the biologists tell us, so our religious and spiritual needs change. And as the psychologists are fond of telling us our needs, our motivations are the prime movers in our lives. So the young today, without reading a word of learned tomes on ancient religions, are manifesting ancient religious rites at the ancient sacred places, because that is what they need to do, and so they are doing it. If you ask them why, for example, they wish to congregate at Stonehenge for the summer solstice, only a very few articulate ones will be able to tell you why, and even they will be fuzzy in their logic and rationale. Because the driving force is not reason or logic, but an unstoppable need to be there then. We are all children of our planet, and for some reason our needs and motivations include the magic of sunrise at a sacred place. It leaves a feeling, it quenches a thirst which cannot be logically explained, but which is none-theless real. Others feel a need to see the sunset at the winter solstice; the last setting of the sun for that year, for the next morning the first sunrise of the next year's sun will rise, only a little way and only for a few hours, but the solstice marks that turning point and there is something truly magical about acknowledging that point and being there and seeing it. It makes you high; it makes you want to sing and dance; it makes you want to shout and run and skip. Hurrah for a new sun (son) is born today. It is not hollow and empty ritual; it is alive and tangible and gives nourishment to the soul and the spirit. And just as our body needs food and water, so does our soul. And this is why so many young people are becoming pagans (Definition of a pagan: one who lives close to Nature.) Our planet needs us to be in tune with her.

Conclusion

The faery faith is a way of life, not a collection of methods. One of the characteristics of this era is supposed to be the enjoyment of life, and joy has always been a key-note of the fair folk. Then there is the faery knowledge and uses of magic, which are just beginning to be accepted by science in the form of parapsychology. Fragmented though it is, the faery lore has a vast store of such knowledge, accumulated through the centuries. The discoveries of modern physics and parapsychology and the old beliefs are so similar that no Inquisitor would notice the differ-ence. Precognition, telepathy, clairvoyance, projecting and activating thought forms, blessing (and cursing) plants or crops are all part of ancient teachings. The human body is a storehouse of energy, which can be put to many uses; this energy can be transmitted by the finger-tips and the hands, as in healing; and the human eyes have dynamic power. Once it would have seemed impossible that faery lore and science could have anything in common; they have come together because of the growing realisation that there is more to life than the five senses tell us of. Modern science is also beginning to realise that there are more senses than the usual five from their research into animals, and from a growing understanding of X-rays, cosmic rays, magnetism, etc.

The belief in the paraphysical world has always existed in a deep layer of the human mind, from which the Victorian philosophies of rationalism and materialism have never actually dislodged it. The more reasonable approach developing today looks on a phenomenon which cannot be explained by known laws as a challenge rather than something to be shunned. The discoveries of modern science relating to the invisible world and its forces can be a means of presenting great spiritual truths in a form in which they can be recognised and used by the majority in over-coming of human problems and in achieving a fuller, more satisfactory way of life. The discoveries of science relating to the psychic world make possible a more rational attitude towards its phenomena. Science is opening to door, which once it slammed shut, to a world in which anything can happen, because it is a world in which mind affects matter, and mind has no discoverable limitations.

As each generation passes so does our spirituality evolve. I feel very excited by the intensely personal mix and matching of the global spiritual theologies that are occurring at the moment. Each person has their own spiritual beliefs and you just cannot have any more religious wars when every person has their own religion! In looking at and attempting to express the so-called new spirituality, I am taking what I have seen to be popular grass root movements as the very things that are of the most importance because they are emerging from people's real needs, despite ourselves – there is no preconceived structure that we are aiming towards – this is what is actually happening to us.

Notes

Chapter 1

[1] Fowler, H.W. & Fowler, F.G. (eds.) (1964).
[2] Kirk, R. (1691/1976).
[3] Dixon, N.F. (1971).
[4] Dixon, N.F. (1981).
[5] Dean, D., Mihalsky, J., Ostrander, S. & Schroeder, L. (1974).
[6] West, D.J. & Fisk, G.W. (1953).
[7] Wiseman, R. & Schlitz, M.J. (1997).
[8] Roney-Dougal, S.M. (1991/2002).
[9] Becker, R.O. (1990).
[10] Burr, H.S. (1972).
[11] Braud, W.G. & Schlitz, M.J. (1991).
[12] May, E.C. et al. (1988).
[13] Baker, R.R. (1981).
[14] Radin, D. (1997).
[15] Betz, H.-D. (1995).
[16] Devereux, P. (1982).
[17] Bord, J. & Bord, C. (1979/1984).
[18] Devereux, P. (1982).
[19] Robins, D. (1988).
[20] Devereux, P. (1990).
[21] Bord, C. & Bord, J. (1972).
[22] Lewis, C.S. (1952/1974).
[23] Reich, W. (ed.) (1960).
[24] Michell, J. (1973).
[25] Peat, D. (1996). Speaking at The Incident Conference at the Institute for Contemporary Arts, London, 11–15th October.
[26] Devereux, P. (1982).
[27] Devereux, P. (1992).
[28] Lessing, D. (1979/1981).
[29] Jones, G & Jones, T. (1949/1982).
[30] Evans Wentz, W.E. (1911/1977).

Chapter 2

[1] Yeats, W.B. (1902/1977), p.2.
[2] Gervase, In Briggs, K. (1967).
[3] Evans Wentz, W.E. (1911/1977).
[4] Fontana, D. (1992).
[5] Evans Wentz, W.E. (1911/1977), p.480.

[6] Morris, R.L. Harary, S.B., Janis, J., Hartwell J. & Roll, W.G. (1978).

[7] Osis, K. & McCormick, D. (1979).

[8] Harpur, P. (1995).

[9] Derr, J.S. & Persinger, M.A. (1989).

[10] Vallée, J. (1970/1975).

[11] Ashe, G. (1990).

[12] Rickard, R.M., Clutching at Straws, In Noyes, R. (ed.) (1991).

[13] Evans Wentz, W.E. (1911/1977).

[14] Harpur, P. (1995). Harpur uses the spelling daimonic which derives from Greek meaning "deity." I prefer daemonic which also derives from Greek and pertains to "myth."

[15] Pratchett, T. (1989).

[16] David-Neel, A. (1965/1971).

[17] Batcheldor, K.J. (1984).

[18] Pratchett, T. (1993a).

[19] Adams, D. (1989).

[20] Vallée, J. (1988/1996).

[21] Blake, W. (1966).

[22] Dunsany, Lord (2001).

[23] Bohm, D. (1982).

[24] Wilber, K. (ed.) (1982).

[25] Talbot, M. (1991/1992).

[26] Schmidt, H. (1976).

[27] Jahn, R.G. & Dunne, B. (1987).

[28] Bohm, D. (1982).

[29] Adams, D. (1989)

Chapter 3

[1] Vallée, J. (1970/1975).

[2] Jung, C. (1959/1977).

[3] Vallée, J. (1988/1996).

[4] Evans, H. (1986).

[5] Devereux, P. (1982).

[6] Evans, H. (1983).

[7] Persinger, M.A. & Lafrenière, G.F. (1977).

[8] Persinger, M.A. & Derr, J.S. (1985).

[9] Devereux, P. (1982).

[10] Fort, C. (1974).

[11] Derr, J.S. (1986).

[12] Persinger, M.A., Ruttan, L.A. & Koren, S. (1990).

[13] Braud, W.G. (1980).

[14] Devereux, P. (1982), p.216.

[15] Sherman, H. (1946).

[16] Koestler, A. (1945).

[17] Vallée, J. (1970/1975).

[18] Evans, H. (1983).

[19] Vallée, J. (1970/1975).

[20] Lovelock, J.E. (1988).

[21] Devereux, P. (1982), p.220.

[22] Vallée, J. (1988/1996).

[23] Porphyry. De Abstinentia, Book II, In Raine, K. & Harper, G.M. (eds.) (1969).

[24] Vallée, J. (1970/1975).

[25] Vallée, J. (1988/1996).

[26] Cheetham, E. (ed.) (1975).

[27] For an example of the Barnum effect in action see: Blackmore, S. (1983).

[28] Tolkien, J.R.R. (1968/1978).

[29] Elworthy, F.T. (1895/1986).

[30] Ker Wilson, B. (1954).

[31] Dunsany, Lord (2001).

[32] Sams, J. & Carson, D. (1988/1999).

[33] Vallée, J. (1988/1996).

[34] Vallée, J. (1970/1975), p.44.

Chapter 4

[1] Gregory, Lady (1920/1979), p.28.

[2] Mitchell, E.D. In White, J. (ed.) (1974).

[3] Jung, C.G. (1964).

[4] Jonas, E. In Ostrander, S. & Schroeder, L. (1971), pp. 350 – 357.

[5] Radin, D. (1997).

[6] Spangler, D. (1971).

[7] Irwin, H. (1985).

[8] Devereux, P. (1992).

[9] Ring, K. (1980).

[10] Jeans, J. In Wilber, K. (ed.) (1984), p.144.

[11] Maslow, A. (1962).

[12] Evans Wentz, W.E. (1911/1977), p.275.

[13] Jung, C.G. (1968).

[14] Rather than using the traditional numbering system of AD and BC, I prefer to use the modern CE which I consider stands for Current Era, and its equivalent BCE, Before Current Era.

[15] Stevenson I. (1987).

[16] Stevenson, I. (1997).

[17] Bohm, D. (1982).

[18] Williams, H. (1978).

Chapter 5

[1] Tart, C.T. (1984).

[2] Roney – Dougal, S.M. (1991/2002).

[3] Committee for the Scientific Investigation of Claims of the Paranormal.

[4] e.g. Pratchett, T. (1989).

[5] e.g. Rowling, J.K. (1997).

[6] Radin, D. (1997).
[7] ibid.
[8] ibid.
[9] Roney-Dougal, S.M. & Solfvin, J. (2002).
[10] Radin, D. (1997).
[11] Deepest gratitude to Keith Bailey who introduced me to this system in 1988, and who has supplied me with calendars for most years since then.
[12] For example, Hole, C. (1978).
[13] Bede, the Venerable (1955).
[14] Wever, R.A. (1979).
[15] Evans Wentz, W.E. (1911/1977).
[16] ibid.
[17] ibid, p.416.

Chapter 6

[1] Stone, M. (1979).
[2] Wilber, K. (ed.) (1982).
[3] Bohm, D. (1982).
[4] Huxley, A. (1946/1974).
[5] A phrase I first heard being used by the Dalai Lama in a talk he gave in London in 1990.
[6] Lovelock, J.E. (1988).
[7] Pribram, K. (1973).
[8] Pribram, K. In Wilber, K. (ed.) (1982).
[9] Wilber, K. (ed.) (1984).
[10] Krippner, S. In Wilber, K. (ed.) (1982).

References

Adams, D. (1989). *The Long Dark Teatime of the Soul*, Pan/Heinemann, Britain.

Anderson, W. (2002). *Green Man: The Archetype of our Oneness with the Earth,* Compass Books, Britain.

Ashe, G. (1990). Mythology of the British Isles, Methuen, Britain.

Baker, R.R. (1981). *Human Navigation & the Sixth Sense.* Hodder & Stoughton, Britain.

Batcheldor, K.J. (1984). Contributions to the theory of PK induction from sitter-group work, *Journal of the American Society for Psychical Research*, 78 (2), 105–122.

Becker, R.O. (1990). *Cross Currents*, Tarcher/Perigee, USA.

Bede, the Venerable (1955). (trans. Shirley-Price, L.) *A History of the English Church and People*, London, Britain.

Betz, H.-D. (1995). Unconventional Water Detection: Field Test of the Dowsing Technique in Dry Zones: Part 1. *Journal of Scientific Exploration*, 9(1), 1–439.

Betz, H.-D. (1995).Unconventional Water Detection: Field Test of the Dowsing Technique in Dry Zones: Part 2. Journal of Scientific Exploration, 9(2), pp.159–189.

Blackmore, S. (1983). Divination with Tarot Cards: An empirical study, *Journal of the Society for Psychical Research*, 52, 97–101.

Blake, W. (1966). (Keynes, G. ed.) *Complete Writings*, Oxford Univ Press, Britain.

Bohm, D. (1982). *Wholeness and the Implicate Order*, Routledge & Kegan Paul, Britain.

Bord, C. & Bord, J. (1972). *Mysterious Britain*, Garnstone Press, Britain.

Bord, J. & Bord, C. (1979/1984). *A Guide to Ancient Sites in Britain*, Paladin, Britain, p.50–51.

Braud, W.G. (1980). Lability and inertia in conformance behaviour, *Journal of the American Society for Psychical Research*, 74, 297–318.

Braud, W.G. & Schlitz, M.J. (1991). Consciousness interactions with remote biological systems: Anomalous intentionality effects. *Journal of Scientific Exploration*, 2(1), 1–46.

References

Briggs, K. (1967). *The Fairies in Tradition and Literature*, London, Britain.

Brookesmith, P. (1995). *UFO: The Complete Sightings Catalogue*, Blandford Press, Britain.

Burr, H. S. (1972). *Blueprint for Immortality: The Electric Pattern of Life*, Neville Spearman, USA.

Carrington, H. (1919). *Modern Psychical Phenomena*, Dodd, Mead & Co., Britain.

Cheetham, E. (ed.) (1975). *The Prophecies of Nostradamus*, Corgi, Britain.

Cooper, R. (1977). *A Guide to British Psilocybin Mushrooms*, Hassle Free Press, Britain.

David-Neel, A.(1965/1971). *Magic and Mystery in Tibet*, Corgi Books, Britain.

Dean, D., Mihalsky, J., Ostrander, S. & Schroeder, L. (1974). *Executive ESP*, Prentice-Hall, USA.

Derr, J.S. (1986). Luminous phenomena and their relationship to rock fracture. *Nature*, 321, 470–471.

Derr, J.S. & Persinger, M.A. (1989). Geophysical variables and behaviour. LIV. Zeitoun (Egypt) apparitions of the Virgin Mary are tectonic strain-induced luminosities. *Perceptual and Motor Skills*, 68, 123–128.

Devereux, P. (1982). *Earth Lights*, Turnstone Press, Britain.

Devereux, P. (1990). *Places of Power*, Blandford Press, Britain.

Devereux, P. (1992). *Shamanism and the Mystery Lines*, Quantum Press, Britain.

Dixon, N.F. (1971). *Subliminal Perception: The Nature of a Controversy*, McGraw Hill, Britain.

Dixon, N.F. (1981). *Preconscious Processing*. Wiley, Britain.

Dunsany, Lord (2001). *The King of Elfland's Daughter*, Gollancz, USA.

Elworthy, F.T. (1895/1986). *The Evil Eye: An Account of this Ancient and Widespread Superstition*, The Julian Press, USA.

Evans, H. (1983). *The Evidence for UFOs*, Aquarian Press, Britain.

Evans, H. (1986). *Visions, Apparitions and Alien Visitors*, Aquarian Press, Britain.

Evans Wentz, W.E. (1911/1977). *The Fairy Faith in Celtic Countries*, Colin Smythe, Gerrards Cross, Britain.

Fontana, D. (1992). The responsive South Wales poltergeist revisited, *Journal of the Society for Psychical Research*, 58, 225–231.

Fort, C. (1974). *The Complete Books of Charles Fort*, Dover Books, USA.

Fowler, H.W. & Fowler, F.G. (eds.) (1964). *The Oxford Dictionary of Current English*, Oxford Univ. Press, Britain.

Frazer, J.G. (1978). *The Illustrated Golden Bough*, Book Club Associates, Britain.

Froud, B. & Lee, A. (1979).*Faeries*, Pan Books, Britain.

Gregory, Lady (1920/1979). *Visions and Beliefs in the West of Ireland*, Colin Smythe, Gerrards Cross, Britain.

Hamilton, G. (1977). *Intention and Survival,* Regency Press, Britain.

Harpur, P. (1995). *Daimonic Reality: Understanding Otherworld Encounters*, Arkana, Britain.

Hole, C. (1978). *A Dictionary of British Folk Customs*, Paladin, Britain.

Hughes, P. (1970). *Witchcraft*, Penguin Books, Britain.

Huxley, A. (1946/1974). *The Perennial Philosophy*, Chatto & Windus, Britain.

Ions, V. (1975). *Egyptian Mythology,* Hamlyn, Britain.

Irwin, H. (1985). *Flight of Mind: A Psychological Study of the Out-of-Body-Experience,* Scarecrow Press, USA.

Jahn, R. G. & Dunne, B. (1987). *Margins of Reality: The Role of Consciousness in the Physical World,* Harcourt Brace Jovanovich, USA.

Jones, G & Jones, T. (1949/1982). *The Mabinogion*, Dragon's Dream, Netherlands.

Jung, C.G. (1964). *Man and His Symbols*, Doubleday, USA.

Jung, C.G. (1968). *The Archetypes and the Collective Unconscious, Collected Works 9, Part 1*, Routledge & Kegan Paul, Britain.

Jung, C. G. (1959/1977). *Flying Saucers: A Modern Myth of Things Seen in the Sky,* Routledge & Kegan Paul, Britain.

Keightley, T. (1850).*The Fairy Mythology*, London, Britain.

Ker Wilson, B. (1954). *Scottish Folk-Tales and Legends*, Oxford University Press, Britain.

Kirk, R. (1691/1976). *The Secret Commonwealth of Elves, Fauns and Fairies; A short treatise of charms and spells*, D. S. Brewer for the Folklore Society, Britain.

Koestler, A. (1945). *The Twilight Bar*, Jonathan Cape, Britain

Lessing, D. (1979/1981). *Shikasta*, Grafton Books, Britain.

Lewis, C.S. (1952/1974). *The Lion, the Witch and the Wardrobe*, Collins, Britain.

Lovelock, J.E. (1988). *The Ages of Gaia*, Oxford Univ. Press, Britain.

References

Maslow, A. (1962). *Toward a Psychology of Being*, Van Nostrand, USA.

May, E. C. *et al.* (1988). Review of the psychoenergetic research conducted at SRI International (1973–1988). *SRI International Technical Report* (March), USA.

McClure, K. (1983). *The Evidence for Visions of the Virgin Mary*, Aquarian Press, Britain.

Michell, J. (1973). *The View over Atlantis*, Abacus, Britain.

Morris, R.L. Harary, S.B., Janis, J., Hartwell J. & Roll, W.G. (1978). Studies of communication during out-of-body experiences, *Journal of the American Society for Psychical Research*, 72, 1–22.

Noyes, R. (ed.) (1991). *The Crop Circle Enigma*, Gateway Books, Britain.

Osis, K. & McCormick, D. (1979). Kinetic effects at the ostensible location of an OB projection during perceptual testing, *Journal of the American Society for Psychical Research*, 74, 319–329.

Ostrander, S. & Schroeder, L. (1971). *Psychic Discoveries Behind the Iron Curtain*, Prentice-Hall, USA.

Peat, D. (1996). *Blackfoot Physics: A Journey into the Native American*, Fourth Estate.

Persinger, M.A. & Derr, J.S. (1985). Geophysical variables and behaviour. XXIII. Relations between UFO reports within the Uinta basin and local seismicity, Perceptual and Motor Skills, 60, 143–152.

Persinger, M.A. & Lafrenière, G.F. (1977). *Space-Time Transients and Unusual Events*, Nelson-Hall, Chicago.

Persinger, M.A., Ruttan, L.A. & Koren, S. (1990). Enhancement of temporal lobe-related experiences during brief exposures to milligauss intensity ELF magnetic field, *Journal of Biochemistry*, 9, 33–45.

Pratchett, T. (1989). *Sourcery*, Corgi, Britain.

Pratchett, T. (1989). *Wyrd Sisters*, Corgi/Bantam, Britain

Pratchett, T. (1993a). *Small Gods*, Corgi/Bantam, Britain.

Pratchett, T. (1993b). *Lords and Ladies*, Corgi/Bantam, Britain.

Pribram, K. (1973). *Psychology of the Frontal Lobes*, Academic Press, NY, USA.

Radin, D. (1997). *The Conscious Universe*, HarperEdge, SanFrancisco, USA.

Raine, K. & Harper, G.M. (eds.) (1969). *Thomas Taylor the Platonist: Selected Writings*, London, Britain.

Reich, W. (ed.)(1960). *Wilhelm Reich: Selected Writings*, Noonday, USA.

Rickard, R.J. & Sieveking, P. (eds.) (1989). *Fortean Times*, 53, 38–45.

Ring, K. (1980). *Life at Death: A Scientific Investigation of the Near-Death Experience,* USA.

Robins, D. (1988). *The Secret Language of Stone,* Rider, Century Hutchinson, Britain.

Roney-Dougal, S.M. (1991/2002). *Where Science & Magic Meet,* Vega Books, Britain.

Roney-Dougal, S.M. & Solfvin, J. (2002). Field Study of Enhancement Effect on Lettuce Seeds – their germination rate, growth and health, *Journal of the Society for Psychical Research,* 66, 129–143.

Rowling, J.K. (1997). *Harry Potter and the Philosopher's Stone,* Bloomsbury, Britain.

Sams, J. & Carson, D. (1988/1999). *Medicine Cards,* St. Martins Press.

Satyananda Saraswati, Sw. (1989). *A Systematic Course in the Ancient Tantric Techniques of Yoga and Kriya,* Bihar School of Yoga, India.

Schmidt, H. (1976). PK effect on pre-recorded targets. *Journal of the American Society for Psychical Research,* 70, 267–292.

Sherman, H. (1946). *The Green Man,* USA.

Spangler, D. (1971). *Revelation, The Birth of a New Age,* Findhorn Publications, Britain.

Spence, L. (1946/1981). *British Fairy Origins: The Genesis and Development of Fairy Legends in British Tradition,* Aquarian Press, Britain.

Stevenson I. (1987). *Children Who Remember Previous Lives,* Univ. Press of Virginia, USA.

Stevenson, I. (1997). *Where Reincarnation and Biology Intersect,* Praeger, USA.

Stone, M. (1979). *The Paradise Papers: The Suppression of Women's Rites,* Virago Press, Britain.

Talbot, M. (1991/1992). *The Holographic Universe,* HarperPerennial, USA.

Tart, C.T. (1984). Acknowledging and dealing with the fear of psi, *Journal of the American Society for Psychical Research,* 78, 133–143.

Tolkien, J. R. R. (1968/1978). *The Lord of the Rings,* Unwin, Britain.

Vallée, J. (1970/1975). *Passport to Magonia: From Folklore to Flying Saucer,* Tandem, Britain.

Vallée, J. (1988/1996). *Dimensions: A Casebook of Alien Contacts,* Souvenir Press, Britain.

West, D. J. & Fisk, G.W. (1953). A dual ESP experiment with clock cards, *Journal of the Society for Psychical Research,* 37, 185–189.

References

Wever, R.A. (1979). *The Circadian System of Man*, Springer-Verlag.

White, J. (ed.) (1974). *Psychic Exploration: A Challenge for Science*, G.P.Putnam, USA.

Wilber, K. (ed.) (1982). *The Holographic Paradigm and Other Paradoxes*, Shambhala, Boulder, USA.

Wilber, K. (ed.) (1984). *Quantum Questions*, Shambhala, Boulder, USA.

Williams, H. (1978). *The Immortalist*, John Calder, Britain.

Wiseman, R. & Schlitz, M.J. (1997). Experimenter effects and the remote detection of staring, *Journal of Parapsychology*, 61, 197–207.

Yeats, W.B. (1902/1977). *Irish Fairy and Folk Tales*, Colin Smythe, Gerrards Cross, Britain.

(1987). *Mysteries of the Unknown: The UFO Phenomenon*, Time-Life Books, USA.

Index

Index

crows, 103, 139

daemonic reality, 49–53, 58, 63, 66, 70, 72, 75, 85, 117
Dalai Lama, 101, 142
dancing, 3, 24–26, 28, 30, 44–48, 76, 93, 126, 132, 136, 148
David Neel, A., 50
death, 30, 39–41, 76, 85, 90, 93, 98, 104–106, 113–114, 131
Defence Mechanism Test, 5
Dean, D., 8
Derr, J.S., 44, 64, 66
devas, 90–91, 136
Devereux, P., 22–25, 32, 59, 64–67, 70, 95
discipline, 50, 122, 136, 152
divination, 4, 31, 34, 81, 94, 142
divinity, 51–55, 82–83, 85–90, 92–95, 97–105, 114, 119, 134, 140–141, 145–146
Dixon, N.F., 7
DMILS, 18, 123
Dragon Project, 22–26
dreams, 3–6, 12, 35, 52–53, 67, 68, 82, 85, 94, 105, 117, 134, 144, 148
Druids, 33, 66, 104, 128
drumming, 3, 51, 148
Dunne, B., 56
Dunsany, Lord, 55, 81
Dunvegan, 80–81

Earthlights hypothesis, 64–67
ectoplasm, 10, 39, 44, 63, 69–70, 82–83, 107
Eddington, A., 151
Einstein, 54–56, 151
electrodermal activity (EDA), 17–18, 123
elementals, 67, 91, 136
elves, 15, 36, 54, 76–82, 91, 111–114
Elworthy, F.Y., 77
emotion, 6, 30
enchantment, 93, 136–137
energy body, 16–20, 30, 40–44, 106–107
EPR paradox. See Bell's theorem
ethics, 120–122, 142–145
Evans, H., 59, 62, 70
Evans Wentz, W.E., 33, 35, 39, 48, 98, 112, 134–136
experimenter effect, 6, 9–10

faery trees
    apple, 93–94
    ash, 26, 144
    elder, 22, 131
    hawthorn, 131, 144
faery food, 71, 98
fairyland. See Otherworld
Faraday chambers, 29, 134
Feng Shui, 31
festivals, 125–133, 147. See also Imbolc, Beltain, Lughnasadh, Samhain
    autumn equinox, 31, 128, 130
    cross-quarter festivals, 129–132
    Easter, 129, 147
    Michaelmas, 128
    midsummer solstice, 92, 128, 154
    spring equinox, 31, 128, 131, 138, 147
    winter solstice, 100, 129, 134, 154
Fianna Faill, 99
Findhorn, 48, 91
Finn Mac Cumhal, 81
Fisk, G.W., 9
Flammarion, 39
follets, 35
Fontana, D., 38
Fort, C., 64
Fortean, 64, 67
Fowler, H.W. & Fowler, F.G., 1

Gaia, 54
Gaia hypothesis, 70, 144
geological fault, 19–26, 44, 64–67
geomagnetic field (GMF), 17–20, 24, 29, 32–34, 44, 64–67, 112, 133
Gervase, 35
ghosts, 20, 30, 50, 53, 57, 106–107
    grey (or white) lady ghost, 39–41, 58, 98
glamour, 3, 124–125
gorsedd, 48
green, 33, 80, 97, 111, 113–114
Green Man, 69, 90, 101, 115
Gregory, Lady, 85
Gwynn Ap Nudd, 2–3, 87, 92, 114, 124

Hallowe'en. See Samhain
Harary, K., 42, 95
Harpur, P., 44, 49
haunting, 20, 22, 30, 37–44, 66, 68, 82–84, 106–107